Presented to:

_____

Presented by:

_____

Date:

_____

Winning 101

DEVOTIONAL

by

Van Crouch

Honor Books
Tulsa, Oklahoma

Winning 101 Devotional
ISBN 1-56292-457-5
Copyright © 1998 by Van Crouch Communications, Inc.
P.O. Box 320
Wheaton, IL 60189

Published by Honor Books
P.O. Box 55388
Tulsa, Oklahoma 74155

Manuscript prepared by W. B. Freeman Concepts, Inc., Tulsa, Oklahoma.

Dedicated to

Ada R. Crouch

A courageous woman of God. Mother, thank-you for keeping your knees bent in prayer and chin up against the winds of adversity. Your example of God's unconditional love convinced me to pursue my dream and fulfill my destiny. Thank you for a lifetime of direction with affection, care, and concern.

In His love and mine,

Van

Introduction

Winning means different things to different people. For some it's power or position. For some it's money. For others, it's the respect of their peers or it's self-satisfaction. For many, winning means having better relationships with the people in their lives.

Most people want to succeed—even people who are negative and pessimistic. We all want to feel we are reaching our full potential. We want to win and feel we are controlling our destiny, that we're not being controlled by it.

Winning is a choice. It means hard work, discipline, and perseverance. To win, you must have a sound strategy as well as short- and long-term goals.

Everyone faces adversity and discouragement. We all go through times when it would be much easier to quit than go forward. At times like this, we need hope beyond the scope of human limitation.

Life-changing truth and hope can be found in the Bible. It is filled with encouraging stories about those who discovered their God-given destiny and pursued it with their whole heart, mind, and soul.

The Bible also contains the truth about how to achieve your dreams and what it means to be a winner in character as well as accomplishment. That's why the devotions in this book are Bible-based. Every motivational quote is coupled with an inspiring verse of Scripture.

The illustrative stories in this book are designed to motivate you to pursue God's plan and purpose for your life, and above all, to keep your eyes on the ultimate goal: eternal life.

Because this inspirational material is grounded in Scripture, it is timeless. It is not the "advice-of-the-day" but rather, "the advice-of-the-ages."

Let God's encouragement sink deep into your heart. Realize the reality that GOD LOVES YOU. He has designed YOU TO WIN in life. STEP UP AND GO FOR IT!

Nobody remembers who came in second.

Do you not know that in a race all the runners run, but only one gets the prize? Run in such a way as to get the prize.

1 Corinthians 9:24

*M*ost people know that Alexander Graham Bell invented the telephone. What is not widely known, however, is that long before Bell's world-changing invention was announced, a German schoolteacher named Reis almost built the telephone. Mr. Reis' phone could carry the sounds of whistling and humming, but it would not transmit human speech. Something seemed to be missing.

Many years later, Bell discovered Reis' error. The adjustment of one small screw that controlled the electrodes was off by one-thousandth of an inch. When Mr. Bell made this minor modification, he was able to transmit speech loud and clear! This infinitesimal distance—an amount few of us could even calculate—made the difference between success and failure.

Today the telephone is an absolute necessity in every home and business. Few inventions in modern history have had such far-reaching ramifications. Bell Labs and the Bell Telephone System are widely known entities. For want of a minor adjustment, the name we all associate with the telephone could have been Reis.

Don't miss the small adjustments you may need to make on your way to success. And don't give up. Keep pursing your goal until you succeed!

■   ■   ■

The man who complains about the way the ball bounces is likely the one who dropped it.

However, I consider my life worth nothing to me, if only I may finish the race and complete the task the Lord Jesus has given me—the task of testifying to the gospel of God's grace.

Acts 20:24

*A*n old fable is told about a hen, a mouse, and a rabbit who lived together in a little house. Because they shared all the work, they lived there happy and content for many years. The rabbit cooked the meals, the chicken carried in the firewood, and the mouse fetched the water from the brook. Each one did his work faithfully.

Then one day while the hen was gathering wood, a busybody crow asked her what she was doing. When the hen told her, the crow informed the hen that she had been strapped with the hardest part of the work. When the hen returned home, she cackled to her companions, "I do the hardest work. We ought to trade jobs."

Her discontent quickly spread and the others agreed to a switch. The rabbit, now assigned to get firewood, hopped into the woods and was immediately eaten by a fox. When the hen put the pail into the creek to get water, she fell in and was drowned. And while attempting to stir the big pot of soup, the mouse fell in and was unable to get out. In their discontent, all three lost not only their joy, but their lives.

Take responsibility for doing your own job to the best of your ability, and you'll be much happier leaving everyone else to do their job.

I can accept failure. Everyone fails at something, but I can't accept not trying.

**I have fought the good fight,
I have finished the race,
I have kept the faith.**

2 Timothy 4:7

*B*asketball superstar Michael Jordan is well-known for his tenacious desire to win. He made the statement on the previous page when he left basketball to try his hand at major-league baseball. Jordan had always desired to play baseball and he didn't want to let his life go by without at least attempting the game.

The key word in Jordan's quote is *accept*. He did not expect failure. To accept and to expect failure are two vastly different concepts.

When he entered the world of baseball, Jordan fully expected to succeed. He knew that the job would be difficult, but he took the challenge anyway. That's the right attitude to have: step up to the challenge and expect not only to work hard, but to succeed.

One thing we must always recognize about success is that it is always linked to suffering of some kind, most often just hard work. Edward Judson once said, "If you succeed without suffering, it is because someone else has suffered before you. If you suffer without succeeding, it is that someone else may succeed after you."

Even if you fail at a task, if you give it your best, your character is strengthened. It also provides an example for others. In the end, your momentary failure will contribute to both your success and the success of those who follow after you.

I'm sorry but we can't use you.

(Coach Walt Keisling to Johnny Unitas after he tried out for the Pittsburgh Steelers.)

These things I have spoken unto you, that in me ye might have peace. In the world ye shall have tribulation: but be of good cheer; I have overcome the world.

John 16:33 *KJV*

*J*ohnny Unitas had been a sandlot football player when he went for a tryout with the Pittsburgh Steelers. The coach, Walt Keisling, said to him, in essence, "Nice try—you have some ability and talent, but you're not for us. We can't use you on our team."

Perhaps Keisling was looking at Unitas' lack of experience. Perhaps Unitas hadn't played up to his potential. Whatever the underlying reason, Unitas didn't allow Keisling's statement to keep him from continuing to pursue his goal. He went to the Baltimore Colts for a tryout, made the team, and went on to great success.

Comedienne Rosie O'Donnell is another winner who didn't let initial rejection keep her from pursuing her goal. From her early days of acting she recalls, "When people would tell me I'm too heavy, too tough, or not pretty enough to succeed, I knew they were wrong. You have to believe in yourself. . . . When I was a kid, I always fantasized my success would be to this degree. My fantasy life was my salvation. It saved me by taking me from where I was to where I wanted to get to."

Has someone told you that you don't have what it takes to be a winner—that you can't be, do, or have what you desire? Refuse to listen to that negative voice, and go on to the next step in your path to victory.

There is no mistake so great as the mistake of not going on.

You were running a good race. Who cut in on you and kept you from obeying the truth?

Galatians 5:7

*M*any of us are familiar with the self-opening gates and cross-arms often found at the entrances and exits of parking lots. What most people don't know is that a variation of this design was used on country roads for many years before it made its way into city use. The gates were a means of controlling the movement of cattle and other animals that grazed on open fields.

The gate would remain closed until a traveler approached it. If the vehicle stopped too far away from the gate, it would not open. But if the vehicle came close enough, its weight pressed the springs below the roadway and the gate would swing open. If the driver stopped before getting all the way through the gate, but had already moved beyond the spring mechanism, the gate was likely to close on him. The driver had to make certain that he went completely through the gate to avoid damage to his vehicle.

This concept readily relates to us today. Regardless of the challenge before us, we must press forward knowing that God will help us succeed. If we fail to give our best effort, the gate may never swing open. If we stop short on the other side, the gate may very well close on us.

Don't be afraid to walk through the gates God opens before you. Walk all the way through to the other side and you'll be on your way to the next one!

■　　■　　■

It ain't over till it's over.

For the which cause I also suffer these things: nevertheless I am not ashamed: for I know whom I have believed, and am persuaded that he is able to keep that which I have committed unto him against that day.

2 Timothy 1:12 KJV

*W*inston Churchill, one of the greatest leaders in history, had a reputation for never quitting. He knew well that losing follows quitting. Those who give up never reach their full potential, and perhaps not even their next goal. One of Churchill's most inspiring statements on the subject was this:

"We shall go to the end, we shall fight in France, we shall fight on the seas and oceans, we shall fight with growing confidence and growing strength in the air, we shall defend our Island whatever the cost may be, we shall fight on the landing grounds, we shall fight in the fields and in the streets, we shall fight in the hills; we shall never surrender, and even if, which I do not for a moment believe, this Island or a large part of it were subjugated and starving, then our Empire beyond the seas, armed and guarded by the British fleet, would carry on the struggle, until, in God's good time, the New World, with all its power and might steps forth to the rescue and the liberation of the old."

Whether it's a war, a game, a business deal, or a fight for one's life, labor to win until the final bell sounds. And after you have done all you can do, pray that others will pick up your effort and press on to even greater heights.

■   ■   ■

People don't care how much you know until they know how much you care.

The third time he said to him, "Simon son of John, do you love me?" Peter was hurt because Jesus asked him the third time, "Do you love me?" He said, "Lord, you know all things; you know that I love you." Jesus said, "Feed my sheep."

John 21:17

*N*apoleon is considered one of the greatest military commanders in all of history. A noted public monument has been erected to him in the city of Paris. But those who perhaps knew Napoleon best—those who lived with him after he was exiled to St. Helena island—would never have raised a monument to him.

Why? Because in many ways, Napoleon was considered a selfish fool.

When Napoleon was exiled, who was there to share his exile? His wife? No. She returned to her father. Was Berthier, his lifelong comrade, there with him? No. He deserted him without even saying good-bye and became a captain in Louis XVIII's guard. Two of Napoleon's trusted marshals openly insulted him. Even the servants who had slept across his bedroom threshold for years left him.

Napoleon lived for himself, and in the end, he died alone.

People want to know that you care. Like Napoleon's friends and family, they don't want to feel they're being used for selfish gain. At the heart of all truly triumphant lives is care and concern for others.

■   ■   ■

Contrary to the cliché, genuinely nice guys most often finish first, or very near it.

He who leads the upright along an evil path will fall into his own trap, but the blameless will receive a good inheritance.

Proverbs 28:10

H. Gordon Selfridge built one of the world's largest department stores in London. He once gave this comparison of the two types of executives. He said:

The boss drives his men.

The leader coaches them.

The boss depends upon authority.

The leader depends on goodwill.

The boss inspires fear.

The leader inspires enthusiasm.

The boss says "I."

The leader, "We."

The boss fixes the blame for the breakdown.

The leader fixes the breakdown.

The boss knows how it is done.

The leader shows how.

The boss says, "Go."

The leader says, "Let's go."

Every person has an opportunity to lead someone at some point in life—perhaps as a parent, a teacher, a minister, a businessman, or a community leader. Choosing to be a leader, rather than a boss, will make you one of the "nice guys" who finishes first!

■   ■   ■

You can make more friends in two months by becoming interested in other people than you can in two years by trying to get other people interested in you.

Give, and it shall be given unto you; good measure, pressed down, and shaken together, and running over, shall men give into your bosom. For with the same measure that ye mete withal it shall be measured to you again.

Luke 6:38 *KJV*

*P*eople love it when they're remembered.

One of the most effective things you can ever do in the business world, as well as in ministry, is to call a person by name. An equally effective technique is to ask questions: How do you feel? What do you think? What is your opinion? How is your family?

In my insurance work I quickly discovered this truth, which I now share with others: million-dollar producers make statements; multimillion-dollar producers ask questions. They ask people what they think and what they desire, and they find a way to respond positively to both.

Find out about another person's hobbies, dreams, goals, desires, beliefs, and ambitions. Then, and only then, will you be able to see the need you—and what you have to offer—can fill.

Mike Murdock says, "What you make happen for others, God will make happen for you." Today, decide to become genuinely interested in others and involve yourself with them. Then, they will naturally become interested and involved with you.

■　　■　　■

You're not finished when you're defeated . . . you're finished when you quit.

But as for you, be strong and do not give up, for your work will be rewarded.

2 Chronicles 15:7

*A*ny person who desires to go far in life is going to face adversity and opportunities to quit. Wanting to quit, having to quit, and quitting voluntarily are three different things. Many times over the years I've experienced the feeling of wanting to quit, but I determined that I would never quit voluntarily.

John Wesley was once denied the privilege of preaching from the pulpit in a particular church. Rather than quit, he used his father's tomb for a pulpit and boldly preached the truths of salvation.

John Knox, another great preacher, often had to be helped to climb the steps into his pulpit, but once there, he preached with divine passion.

Still another great preacher, George Whitefield, returned from a preaching tour extremely weary one night. He lit a candle and prepared to climb the stairs to his bedroom; then he noticed that a group of people had gathered in front of his house. He invited them into his foyer, and lit candle in hand, preached his last message from the stairway. He died in his sleep that night.

If you want to win, stay in the game. It's always too soon to quit.

■ ■ ■

The superior man is modest in his speech, but exceeds in his actions.

Teach me, and I will hold my tongue: and cause me to understand wherein I have erred.

Job 6:24 *KJV*

A father and his son went into the wheat fields at harvesttime. As they looked across the waving golden grain, the boy said, "Father, look at how these wheat heads hold themselves up so proudly. They must be the ones filled with the most grain."

"No, my son," the father replied. And he took some of the heads that stood up so proudly and crushed them in his hands. They yielded only a few poor, shriveled grains. He explained, "Those who bow their heads humbly are the ones filled with large, golden kernels of wheat."

Many people talk the talk of faith, but they don't walk the walk. They don't bear the fruit of their faith. They avoid situations where they would have to put their words into action.

The true walk of faith is a walk of humility—of submitting oneself to the Lord. The walk of humility is not contrary to the pursuit of excellence. Rather, it is trusting in God to help one persevere and arrive at His goals for their life, which are always excellent.

God is not in the humbling business. He tells us in His Word that we must humble ourselves. God will never force us. We must trust Him and walk and talk in obedience to His voice.

The four-way test of the things we think, say, or do: Is it the truth? Is it fair to all concerned? Will it build goodwill and better relationships? Will it be beneficial to all concerned?

Finally, brethren, whatsoever things are true, whatsoever things are honest, whatsoever things are just, whatsoever things are pure, whatsoever things are lovely, whatsoever things are of good report; if there be any virtue, and if there be any praise, think on these things.

Philippians 4:8 KJV

The Rotary International motto (quoted at left), which has gone around the world and impacted millions of people, truly presents a "winning" way to live.

Taking others into consideration brings up the issue of fairness—do we speak and act so that all involved will benefit? Are we concerned not only with our own victory but with helping others to win alongside us?

We are commanded by God to speak the truth in love. Speaking the truth in love means to only give the information that is absolutely necessary to the good outcome of the situation. We all know that gossip is rooted in rumor and half-truth. Yet even if something is true, it may not need to be said—especially if it will bring harm to an innocent person.

If we speak only the truth, and only that truth which needs to be spoken, with the proper attitude, we will build goodwill and better relationships with others. When goodwill and affinity with others are firmly established, what we do will be beneficial to all concerned because we will be careful not to do harm to anyone.

In all things—and especially in your conversation—always speak the truth in love, keeping others at the forefront of your mind and your heart.

It's what you learn after you know it all that counts.

Shew me thy ways, O LORD;
teach me thy paths.

Psalm 25:4 KJV

A young man often had occasion to walk by the home of a well-respected professor in his community. He noticed that most of the time as he passed the professor's home, whether early in the morning or late at night, he could see the professor poring over books in his study.

One day he had an opportunity to talk to the professor and he asked him, "Doctor, I'd like to know, what is it that keeps you studying? You are at the top in your field—a full professor with many opportunities to speak at major universities. Yet, you never seem to stop learning."

The professor replied, "Son, I would rather have my students drink from a running stream than from a stagnant pool."

John Wooden, who established an incredible coaching record at UCLA, was of the same opinion. He believed that we must never stop learning and growing— what we continue to learn will only make us richer, sweeter, and deeper.

The wonderful thing about the Word of God is that no matter how many thousands of times a person reads it, there's always something new to learn from it. Take a daily drink from the wellspring of all learning and wisdom—the Bible. Its truths will make you a champion!

■   ■   ■

Don't ever talk until you know what you're talking about.

Let the words of my mouth and the meditation of my heart be acceptable in Your sight, O LORD, my strength and my Redeemer.

Psalm 19:14 NKJV

*T*wo men once went up in a hot-air balloon and became lost. They finally spotted a man on the ground so they descended within shouting distance, hoping he might be able to give them some direction.

One man leaned over the edge of the basket and shouted, "Could you please tell us where we are?"

The man on the ground replied, "Yes, you are in a balloon about fifty feet in the air."

The man in the balloon said to his partner, "Let's move on and try to find someone who isn't a CPA."

His friend asked, "How do you know he's a CPA?"

He said, "Because he gave us completely accurate information which was of absolutely no value to us!"

Often we can get so wrapped up in the details and particulars of what we want to say that we fail to consider our audience. If we want to sound as if we know what we are talking about, we first must know to whom we are speaking and what they need to know. Anything we say that lies beyond their needs and their interests is going to sound like babbling.

While it is important to know what you are talking about, it is even more critical to know to whom you are speaking. Information without application is of little use to anybody.

All of us must become better informed. It is necessary for us to learn from others' mistakes. You will not live long enough to make them all yourself.

You therefore, beloved, since you know this beforehand, beware lest you also fall from your own steadfastness . . . grow in the grace and knowledge of our Lord and Savior Jesus Christ.

2 Peter 3:17-18 *NKJV*

A school principal once protested to his superintendent because he wasn't given a certain promotion he thought he deserved. "After all," he argued to his superior, "I've had twenty-five years of experience."

The superintendent replied, "No, Joe, that's where you're wrong. You have had one year's experience twenty-five times."

Repeating the same lessons over and over again is not a means to personal growth. Generally speaking, we need to get beyond ourselves in our learning. We need to study those who have succeeded in life to learn what to do and what not to do. The legendary insurance man from East Liverpool, Ohio, Ben Feldman, once said, "Only a fool learns from his own experience."

What we learn from others can help us avoid pitfalls and make wise decisions. Select your own "life board of directors," people who will speak truth into your life. Choose a competent pastor and Bible teacher from whom you can learn more about God's Word. Read books both by and about great men and women.

To be a winner, choose to learn from winners.

Character is what a man is in the dark.

A double minded man is unstable in all his ways.

James 1:8 *KJV*

"The truth will come out." "Hidden things always come to light." These familiar phrases point to the same truth: your character will eventually reveal itself.

The person of good character won't just speak the truth in public; he'll speak the truth to himself in private. He won't even consider something like adjusting figures on his income tax forms to reflect a lie.

The person of good character won't only advocate morality in public, he will closely monitor all of his own moral choices. He won't even consider watching an inappropriate movie, even when he is in the privacy of a motel room far from home.

The person of good character won't only demonstrate his faith in public, he will choose to become a disciplined person of faith in his private life—praying regularly even if nobody knows, reading the Scriptures even when his schedule is busy.

Character is not something that can be developed in moments of crisis. It is developed in secret, over time—one decision at a time.

A genuine winner is a person of good character. Decide today to make the choices necessary to develop your own character, because the person of poor character has already lost the most important game.

■   ■   ■

The time is always right to do what is right.

To him that soweth righteousness shall be a sure reward.

Proverbs 11:18 KJV

*D*r. Madison Sarratt, who taught mathematics at Vanderbilt University for many years, often had this to say to his classes before he gave them an exam:

"Today I am giving two examinations—one in trigonometry and the other in honesty. I hope you will pass them both.

"If you must fail one of the exams, fail trigonometry. There are many good people in the world who cannot pass trig, but there are no good people in the world who cannot pass the examination of honesty."

Doing what is wrong always brings about some type of negative consequence. There may not be any immediate outward punishment or bad fortune, but wrongdoing always generates something in the soul which—unless it is repented of—will become the seed for yet another act of wrongdoing. Eventually, outward consequences will result.

By the same divine law, doing what is right always brings about positive consequences. The visible signs of blessing may take awhile to appear, but eventually they will.

■　　■　　■

There is no real excellence in all this world which can be separated from right living.

Righteousness exalteth a nation: but sin is a reproach to any people.

Proverbs 14:34 *KJV*

A wealthy man once purchased a famous painting of Jesus for a very large sum of money. He then struggled to find an appropriate place in his home to hang the painting. At last he called in an architect for advice. The architect studied his home and his painting with great care and then said, "Sir, you cannot fit this picture into your home. You must make a home to fit it."

We err anytime we ask God to allow us to live our lives the way we want to live them. The correct approach is to seek to live our lives the way God wants us to live them.

That was certainly the approach that John Wanamaker took. He once was asked, "How do you find time to run a Sunday school with four thousand in attendance, run the business of your stores, work as postmaster general, and fulfill all of your other civic and family obligations?" Wanamaker replied, "Sunday school is my business! All other things are just things. Forty-five years ago I decided that God's promise was sure: 'Seek ye first the kingdom of God, and his righteousness; and all these things shall be added unto you (Matthew 6:33 KJV).'"

Make right living your supreme business and you will be guaranteed a place in the winner's circle.

From time immemorial, God's problem has been to get men to look from His viewpoint.

For I am persuaded, that neither death, nor life, nor angels, nor principalities, nor powers, nor things present, nor things to come, Nor height, nor depth, nor any other creature, shall be able to separate us from the love of God, which is in Christ Jesus our Lord.

Romans 8:38-39 *KJV*

While a preacher was busy in his study one morning, his young son was nearby looking at a picture book. The man realized he needed a large book that he had left upstairs and he asked his son to get it for him. The boy was away for a long time, and after awhile the father heard the sound of sobbing coming from the staircase. He left the study and found his son at the top of the stairs, crying. The large book which he had tried to carry was lying at his feet. He sobbed, "Oh, Daddy, I can't carry it. It's too heavy for me."

In a flash, the father ran up the stairs and picked up both the book and his son in his strong arms, and carried them both to the study below.

On Sunday the preacher related the story, saying, "And that is how God deals with His children."

We often think of God as a fierce judge, ready to punish us for the slightest error. In reality, if we could only see things from God's perspective, we would see He is a loving Father eager to forgive us when we turn to Him. It is precisely when our load of guilt and shame becomes heavy, or life's responsibilities cause us to become weary, that He desires to lift us up in His arms.

Turn to God today for the forgiveness, strength, and comfort you need.

We trust, sir, that God is on our side. It is more important to know that we are on God's side.

For the eyes of the LORD range throughout the earth to strengthen those whose hearts are fully committed to him.

2 Chronicles 16:9

*N*oted minister Dr. F. B. Meyer had come to a crossroads in his ministry. Feeling dejected, he said out loud to no one in particular, "My ministry is unfruitful, and I lack spiritual power." He felt completely helpless. He had no idea what to do.

Suddenly, he realized Jesus was standing beside him. "Let Me have the keys to your life," He seemed to say. The experience was so real to Meyer that he reached into his pocket and took out his key ring.

"Are all the keys here?" the Lord asked. "Yes, Lord, all except the key to one small room in my life," Meyer admitted.

"If you cannot trust Me in all the rooms of your life, I cannot accept any of the keys," the Lord said. At that, Meyer was so overwhelmed by the feeling that Jesus was walking away from him, that he cried, "Come back, Lord, and take the keys to all the rooms in my life!"

That experience proved to be a turning point in Meyer's ministry. From that time on, his preaching became significantly more powerful and effective.

I realized years ago that it was important for me to say, "I know God and I trust Him with my life." But, I concluded, it is far more important that God say at the end of my life, "I know Van, and I trust him with My life." Are you on God's side today?

■ ■ ■

Issues of life and death can be decided upon only by people who are willing to do their homework and develop their insights and opinions through seeking God's kingdom.

Therefore came I forth to meet thee, diligently to seek thy face, and I have found thee.

Proverbs 7:15 KJV

*M*ike Singletary was a great, all-pro middle linebacker—number 50 for the Chicago Bears. He was not the biggest nor the most talented player to play his position, but Mike exhibited these great qualities which made him a winner:

- A thorough knowledge of the game of football.

- A record of doing his homework—he spent hours watching game films and digging deep for facts about his opponents.

- Steady leadership every day, to every person he encountered.

These are traits any person can develop to become a winner, regardless of his or her profession.

Many professional athletes are heroes on the field and zeros off the field. Mike is not one of them. He is a strong Christian, a winner at home with his wife and five children, a leader in his community, and now, a noted public speaker who inspires thousands of people each year in the corporate arena.

Today, ask God to help you follow Mike's example. Become an expert in your field, dig for insights that will lead you to success, and be a positive witness to everyone you encounter. Don't just have a fabulous career, have a fabulous life!

■ ■ ■

Take calculated risks. That is quite different from being rash.

For which of you, intending to build a tower, does not sit down first and count the cost, whether he has enough to finish it.

Luke 14:28 NKJV

William of Ockham, who lived in England about six hundred years ago, was a graduate of Oxford University and was considered one of the most brilliant men of his day.

William became entangled in church politics, however, advocating that the church should confine itself to spiritual matters and stay out of the government. He caused such a commotion that the powers he was criticizing decided to get rid of him. He learned of their plot and escaped to a distant land. Once there, he developed a tool that later came to be known as Ockham's Razor.

The Razor of Ockham is not a tool per se, but rather, a method of thinking that cuts directly to the core of any problem, removing all unnecessary facts from the subject being analyzed. Ockham's Razor was his ability to see the bare bones of a problem.

This skill is not only highly prized in business today, but can be the key difference between "taking a risk" and "being rash." Risk-taking should always be based upon good information, thoughtful strategy, and clear perception.

You can apply this principle to every situation you face today. Remember: Jesus told us to "count the cost," and He freely gives us the wisdom to do so.

Lord, deliver me from the man who never makes a mistake, and also from the man who makes the same mistake twice.

This one thing I do, forgetting those things which are behind, and reaching forth unto those things which are before, I press toward the mark for the prize of the high calling of God in Christ Jesus.

Philippians 3:13-14 *KJV*

A number of years ago Liddell Hart, a noted British military expert, liked to tell the story of a young man in New York City who spent an entire week going from store to store to store. His purpose? To change a dollar bill into two fifty-cent pieces, the two fifty-cent pieces into quarters, the quarters into dimes, the dimes into nickels, and the nickels into pennies.

After he had exchanged his dollar into one hundred pennies, he reversed the process, going from store to store to exchange pennies for nickels, nickels for dimes, dimes for quarters, and so forth.

When he had gone through this strange procedure three times, Hart asked him why he was doing such a strange thing. The young man smiled craftily and said, "One of these days, somebody is going to make a mistake —and it isn't going to be me!"

While it is important to do one's best and not make mistakes out of laziness, sloppiness, or lack of information, it is even more important to do a job that is meaningful. Meaningful work causes both you and those around you to grow.

Choose to take risks. You may make mistakes, but when you do, learn from them and commit yourself to not repeating them. Winners are not error-free—they are error-aware.

When I am secure in Christ, I can afford to take a risk in my life. Only the insecure cannot afford to risk failure. The secure . . . can admit failure . . . seek help and try again.

For He made Him who knew no sin to be sin for us, that we might become the righteousness of God in Him.

2 Corinthians 5:21 *NKJV*

*H*ow can Christ give us the security to risk failure, admit failure, seek help, and try again? Because He strengthens us through His unconditional love. He loves us because He chooses to love us, not because of our performance or achievement.

When you know you are loved based on who you are, and not on what you have done or are doing, you have the ultimate in self-esteem—a self-esteem born of God's esteem for you! You never have to fear failure because Christ is always there, ready to forgive you, help you, and renew you.

Consider the many times you have failed. You fell down the first time you tried to walk. You probably almost drowned the first time you tried to swim. In all likelihood, you didn't hit a home run the first time you picked up a baseball bat. Failure in our lives is certain.

All of the great achievers in history have failed. R. H. Macy failed seven times before his New York department store caught on. Babe Ruth struck out 1,330 times—almost twice as many times as he hit a home run. English novelist John Creasy received 753 rejection slips before his first book was published, and he went on to have 563 more books published.

You may fail, but Christ never labels you a failure. In Him, having received His forgiveness and love, you are always a winner, not only now but forever!

■   ■   ■

*You can spend
your life any way
you want to,
but you can
only spend
it once.*

**It is appointed unto men once to die,
but after this the judgment.**

Hebrews 9:27 KJV

*A*n oil company in Indonesia once asked a local missionary to go to work for them. They offered him a large salary, so they were surprised when he declined. They said, "Just name your salary. We'll pay it." He replied, "Oh, the salary is big enough, but the job isn't big enough."

As free moral agents, God has given each of us the privilege to make decisions about our lives and how we will spend our time and energy. God does not dictate the way we must live. He tells us how we should live, and then leaves the decision up to us.

When I was in the insurance business, I often told my prospects, "When they back that hearse up to the front door, they aren't making a practice run. Mortality is running one out of one. Take a look at this insurance policy and call me in the morning—if you wake up."

On more than one occasion, a prospect said to me, "You're just trying to pressure me." My response was, "No, I'm just trying to get you to wake up and see the urgency of deciding something today." The decisions we make each day become the direction of our future.

The old hymn proclaims, "Only one life will soon be past—only what's done for Christ will last."

Choose a job that's big enough—then do it now.

■ ■ ■

It is not enough to be busy; so are the ants. The question is: What are we busy about?

And [Jesus] said unto them, How is it that ye sought me? wist ye not that I must be about my Father's business?

Luke 2:49 *KJV*

*W*hen multimillionaire financier J. P. Morgan died, he left a will that contained 10,000 words and thirty-seven articles. During his lifetime, Morgan made countless financial transactions, some of which impacted the economic equilibrium of the entire world. Yet in his will, he wrote about the one transaction he considered supreme above all others:

"I commit my soul in the hands of my Saviour, full of confidence that, having redeemed me and washed me with His most precious blood, He will present me faultless before the throne of my Heavenly Father.

"I entreat my children to maintain and defend, at all hazard and at any cost of personal sacrifice, the blessed doctrine of complete atonement of sins through the blood of Jesus Christ once offered, and through that alone."

Although one of the busiest men in history, Morgan had the right priorities, the right purpose. A noted Italian economist came up with the "law of inverse production," which simply means, "twenty percent of your input yields 80 percent of your output." Choose to be busy about the right things, and for the right purpose, and you will get the right results.

What can you do today to take your life to the next level? What should you be busy doing?

■　　■　　■

*God has given me
this day to use as
I will . . . what I do
today is important,
because I am
exchanging a day
of my life for it!*

**Forsake the foolish, and live;
and go in the way of understanding.**

Proverbs 9:6 *KJV*

An old legend is told about a young man who was greatly beloved by his family. He died, and in the afterlife he petitioned God to let him return to the world for just one day so that he might relive it. He didn't ask to relive the best day of his life, but rather, the day that was least notable and most ordinary. God granted his request and he instantly appeared in his old home, everything just as it was when he was fifteen years old. As the young man entered the living room, his mother passed by him. She was busy doing a household chore and didn't even seem to be aware of his presence. When he stepped out into the yard, he saw his father striding across the yard carrying tools in his hand. Intent on his task, he gave his son an indifferent glance and passed him by.

The young man concluded, "Why, we are all dead most of the time! The only ones who are truly alive are those who are conscious of the treasure that we have in our friends and loved ones." And with that, he asked to be returned to heaven, where he knew that every person was cherished every moment.

Today, focus on those who are in your life now. God has given you a day as the supreme unit of time to use for Him. What, or who, is worthy of your day today?

■   ■   ■

Imagination is more important than knowledge.

To all that be in Rome, beloved of God, called to be saints: Grace to you and peace from God our Father, and the Lord Jesus Christ.

Romans 1:7 *KJV*

A number of years ago, a popular advertisement showed a boy gazing into the future. In the background a planet was whirling and a rocket was bursting into outer space. The heading for the ad said, "You're as big as you think!" The caption then went on to read:

"Only a boy. But his thoughts are far in the future. Thinking, dreaming, his mind sees more than his eyes do. So with all boys . . . vision, looking beyond the common place, finds new things to do. And growth, as it always must, follows where mind marks the way."

What do you dream about? What has God enabled you to see that does not yet exist?

God created you with an imagination. He gave you the ability to dream, to have faith for things which do not yet exist, and to attain high goals. In fact, it is part of your being made in God's image, for God has an imagination of His own. He has daydreams. Some of what He has dreamed turned out to be you.

If God were rewriting this old ad, He'd likely picture you with the heading, "You're only as big as your imagination!"

If you can dream it, you can do it. . . . This whole thing was started by a mouse.

And the LORD answered me, and said, Write the vision, and make it plain upon tables, that he may run that readeth it.

Habakkuk 2:2 KJV

*I*s there a person alive who hasn't heard about Mickey Mouse or Disney World? What we must remember is that all of the things associated with Disney began with a dream in the mind of one man—Walt Disney.

The story is told of another dreamer, a young Scottish boy, who was sleeping in the heather beside a brook one day. In his dream, the sky became filled with a dazzling golden light. Out of the light, a chariot appeared, drawn by horses of fire.

Faster and faster the horses descended from the sky. When the chariot came near the boy, he heard a powerful voice gently say, "Come up here. I have work for you to do." The boy stood to obey, and as he did, he awoke and realized he had been dreaming.

Did he discount this dream? No. That night he went into his room, knelt by his bed, and prayed, "O Lord, You know I don't have any silver or gold. All I have is myself. Will You accept me as a gift?" And he rose with great assurance that God had heard his prayer and accepted him. He determined to become a missionary and share the good news of God's acceptance with others. His dream led him to become one of the greatest missionaries in India's history.

Whatever the dream God has given you, act on it! Where God calls, He always provides—the power, strength, energy, finances, and courage you need to fulfill the dream.

■   ■   ■

The only thing that stands between a man and what he wants from life is often merely the will to try it and the faith to believe that it is possible.

But without faith it is impossible to please him: for he that cometh to God must believe that he is, and that he is a rewarder of them that diligently seek him.

Hebrews 11:6 *KJV*

*R*ichard De Vos and Jay Van Andel began the Amway Corporation out of their garages with the belief that it was possible to start small and build something great. They had faith in God who gave them their ability, and thus, faith in their ability.

The beginning of anything great in your life is likely to come when you say, "I can do something with my life." You must see the options. You must have a knowing deep inside you that you can be more.

Then, you must find something that captures your interest—something about which you care deeply. That something will be the focus for your energy.

English novelist J. B. Priestly was once asked how he had become a famous writer, while several very gifted writers with whom he had associated as a youth had not matured in their skills. He gave this answer: "The difference between us was not in ability, but in the fact that they merely toyed with the fascinating idea of writing. I cared like blazes! It is this caring like the blazes that counts."

Do you believe in the fire that God has kindled within you? Do you care "like blazes" about something? Then burn the midnight oil with your own zeal and God's wisdom and go about making your dream a reality.

Don't let anyone steal your dream!

*The LORD will fulfill his purpose for me;
your love, O LORD, endures forever—
do not abandon the works of your hands.*

Psalm 138:8

William Carey was often called a foolish, impractical dreamer for studying foreign languages and the travelogs of Captain Cook. Those who knew him when he was a cobbler scoffed at the large map he kept on the wall of his workshop so he might pray for the nations of the world throughout the day.

Even after he became a minister, Carey was considered foolish for presenting this topic for discussion at a ministers' conference: "Whether or not the Great Commission is binding upon us today to go and teach all nations." An older minister rebuked him, saying, "Sit down, young man. When God pleases to convert the heathen, He will do it without your aid or mine!"

Carey was silenced for the moment, but not stopped. He went on to become a pioneering missionary in India.

Someone will always emerge to try to steal your dream. It may be someone who is on welfare, doesn't have a job, left school in the fifth grade, and considers his fishing license his best form of ID! It may be a relative who continually hounds you with what God "can't do, wouldn't do, and shouldn't do" through you. Never, never, never let a person who is a cop-out, burnout, or dropout cause you to give up the dream that God has put in your heart!

God has destined you to triumph!

You are about to experience a turning point. Stay in the game—it's too soon to quit.

Jesus said to them, "My food is to do the will of Him who sent Me, and to finish His work."

John 4:34 *NKJV*

A survey once made by the National Retail Dry Goods Association revealed these surprising facts about salespeople:

- 48 percent make one call and quit,
- 25 percent make two calls and quit,
- 15 percent make three calls and quit.

Some 88 percent of all salespeople quit attempting to sell something to a prospect after calling on them three times or less! Fortunately, some of them make a sale during their first, second, or third call—but their combined total sales amount only to about 20 percent of all that is sold.

What about the other 12 percent? They keep calling, and they end up doing 80 percent of the business! Most of the business becomes a written order after the fourth contact.

The storms of life may dissuade you from pressing forward. Always remember that storms come for a reason, and they come only for a season. Discover what you are to learn through a storm and then weather it out. Don't let the storm keep you from sailing onward.

■ ■ ■

Some of us let these great dreams die, but others nourish and protect them, nurse them through bad days till they bring them to the sunshine and light which come always.

On the same day, when evening had come, He said to them, "Let us cross over to the other side."

Mark 4:35 NKJV

*A*s I have traveled our nation, I have discovered that many people don't seem to dream. I feel certain that they dreamed as children, but somehow, as they became involved in the humdrum of life they let their dreams die.

Marriage counselors often see this happen with couples in love. A marriage starts with great plans, great romance, and great bliss. But then the relationship seems to grind to a halt in the mire of the mundane.

A dream, as a marriage, must be nourished if it is to survive. One of the best ways I know to keep a dream alive is to talk about it—but only with someone who has done what you want to do or who has paid the price you are willing to pay. Never talk about your dream to someone who has no dreams of their own or doesn't believe you can reach yours.

As you grow and mature, God will reveal more of your dream and you will begin to see the big picture. Over time, you may have to amend your dreams. Even so, continue to believe in what God has planted in your heart. He would not have called you to the "other side" if He had not intended for you to arrive there!

Jesus had a purpose in getting to the other side of the stormy lake—to bring deliverance to a demon-filled man. God has a purpose in your arriving also—and it will always include blessing someone in need.

■　　■　　■

Dreams are the touchstones of our character.

For as he thinketh in his heart, so is he.

Proverbs 23:7 *KJV*

*S*leep and dream studies conducted over a ten-year period by Boston researcher Dr. Ernest Hartmann, revealed that those who need more than nine hours of sleep a night are worriers who tend to mull over their problems in their dreams. Those who sleep fewer than six hours tend to be efficient people who push problems aside and continue to pursue their goals—people like Thomas Edison and Albert Einstein.

Dr. Hartmann concluded, "Great [people] in the sense of extremely effective, practical persons—administrators, applied scientists, political leaders, perhaps—may tend to be short sleepers."

The difference in what kind of sleep each group of people gets seems to lie in how much they dream. Those who sleep long get two to three times as much REM (rapid eye movement) sleep, the deep sleep in which dreams occur. Dr. Hartmann has speculated that they need this extra dream sleep to resolve deep-seated mental and emotional needs.[1]

How can we apply this to our quest to be winners? If you pursue your dreams in every waking moment, you will not have to spend your dreamtime worrying about your lack of success!

Most men exchange their lifetime for much too little. Don't be afraid to think big.

Then Saul said to David, "May you be blessed, my son David; you will do great things and surely triumph." So David went on his way, and Saul returned home.

1 Samuel 26:25

*O*ne day, the great artist Michelangelo went into the studio of Raphael and looked at one of his early drawings. Then he took a piece of chalk and wrote the word "Amplius," which means "greater" or "larger," across the entire drawing. Michelangelo could see in an instant that Raphael's sketch was too cramped, too narrow in its vision. He encouraged Raphael to think bigger, to have a larger vision for his work.[2]

For years, Oral Roberts—founder, former president, and now chancellor of Oral Roberts University—has had a plaque on his desk. It reads: "Make No Little Plans Here."

It was this type of thinking that led him not only to become an internationally-recognized evangelist, but to found an institution of higher learning—and not a no-name, unaccredited school, but a fully accredited university with several graduate schools. Oral Roberts University now has thousands of alumni who can be found literally around the world.

It was this type of thinking that led him to go on radio with his Gospel message, and then to television, and then to the building of a television network.

How big is your vision today? Are your goals, dreams, and plans big enough?

■   ■   ■

Any man who selects a goal in life which can be fully achieved has already defined his own limitations.

Jesus said unto him, If thou canst believe, all things are possible to him that believeth.

Mark 9:23 *KJV*

*A*fter Robert Taft was defeated by Dwight D. Eisenhower for the Republican nomination for president in 1952, a reporter asked him about his personal and professional goals.

Taft replied, "My great goal was to become president of the United States in 1953." The reporter smirked as he asked, "Well, you didn't make it, did you?"

"No," Taft admitted without the least bit of embarrassment or chagrin, "but I became a senator from Ohio!"[3]

Think of your goal as a dartboard. The bull's-eye equals 100. The concentric rings are 80, 60, 40, 20. If you aim for the bull's-eye, you may often hit it. At other times, you may hit 80 or even 20. But if you don't aim for 100, you'll probably hit zero every time. Someone once said, "I would rather attempt to do something great for God and fail, than to do nothing and succeed."

Today, see yourself as an achiever, a winner, an overcomer, a conqueror. Aim to fulfill the picture you see! Go for the very best you can imagine. Even if you fall short of your goal, you'll achieve far more than you will if you have no dreams or goals at all.

Be a dreamer. If you don't know how to dream, you're dead.

If . . . you seek the LORD your God, you will find him if you look for him with all your heart and with all your soul.

Deuteronomy 4:29

*J*im Valvano, former coach at North Carolina State, made this statement to a reporter on national television while he was dying of bone cancer. Even in the face of death, Valvano had an eye toward what might still be done.

Ideas that propel us forward in the pursuit of our dreams often come from unlikely sources. Unless we are looking for answers, we may miss them.

As Eli Whitney toured the South more than a century ago, cotton growers told him how difficult it was to extract seeds from raw cotton. "If only," they said, "someone could devise a machine to do that work!"

That night Whitney lay awake thinking about their problem. Long after midnight, he arose and went to the window of his room for a breath of fresh air. He looked down on the farmyard below and saw that a cat had killed a chicken and was desperately trying to pull it out of the coop. He couldn't succeed, however, because the space between the slats of the coop was too narrow.

Then the thought occurred to him: Why not build an iron claw that would pull the cotton fibers through a fine mesh, leaving the hard seeds behind? Within a week, he had sketched plans for the first cotton gin.[4]

The answers to the problems you encounter can often be found in your dreams. Keep your eyes open and believe that God will show you the solutions you need.

Keep dreaming and keep doing!

■   ■   ■

Most men die from the neck up at age twenty-five because they stop dreaming.

Where there is no vision, the people perish.
Proverbs 29:18 *KJV*

*T*he Minnesota Medical Association defines an "old" person as a person who:

- feels old,
- feels he has learned all there is to learn,
- finds himself saying, "I'm too old for that,"
- feels that tomorrow holds no promise,
- takes no interest in the activities of youth,
- would rather talk than listen,
- longs for the "good old days."

By this definition, I know a great many people who are old at the age of thirty!

General Douglas MacArthur once said:

"Nobody grows old by merely living a number of years. People grow old only by deserting their ideals. Years may wrinkle the skin, but to give up interest wrinkles the soul. Worry, doubt, self-distrust, fear, and despair . . . these are the long, long years that bow the head and turn the growing spirit back to dust.

"You are as young as your faith, as old as your doubt; as young as your self-confidence, as old as your fear; as young as your hope, as old as your despair."[5]

Choose to stay young. It's all in your attitude. When you choose to stay young, it's a sign you are still capable of growth!

I do not fear failure. I only fear the "slowing up" of the engine inside of me which is pounding, saying, "Keep going, someone must be on top, why not you?"

For You have armed me with strength for the battle; You have subdued under me those who rose up against me.

Psalm 18:39 *NKJV*

*T*he most courageous team in the history of college football may be the University of Sewannee squad of 1899. With only five more games left to play that season, they were undefeated. The remaining games, however, were scheduled over a six-day period, and against five of the most powerful teams in the nation. Furthermore, these teams were located in five different cities many miles apart, long before the days of jet travel!

Sewannee defeated Texas University 12-0 in the first game. The next day, after traveling by horse and wagon and with little rest, they destroyed Texas A&M 32-0. After another long ride by wagon, they played their third game in three days, this time against Tulane University. Sewannee won 23-0.

The fourth day was Sunday so the squad took a day off for prayer and rest. The next day they downed undefeated Louisiana State University 34-0. The following day they beat Mississippi State 12-0. Not one of these five powerhouses scored a single point against Sewannee, who by the way, played with only eleven men and no substitutes![6]

So what's your excuse for quitting before you've reached your championship?

In the space age the most important space is between the ears.

Do not be conformed to this world, but be transformed by the renewing of your mind, that you may prove what is that good and acceptable and perfect will of God.

Romans 12:2 *NKJV*

When a group of scientists was asked to determine the size, cooling system, and power required to perform the same functions automatically accomplished by a person's brain during his lifetime, they concluded that one would need: "A machine the size of the United Nations building in New York, a cooling system with output equal to Niagara Falls, and a power source that produced as much electricity as is used in homes and industry in the entire state of California."

Another scientist calculated that although the average person's brain is incapable of bringing to the conscious mind more than 90 percent of what it learns during a lifetime, the brain is still capable of storing more than ten times the information contained in the Library of Congress—more than 20 million volumes![7]

Your mind is the most important resource you have. Use it well. Don't let it become dominated by the media or doomsayers. Go to the Word of God and see what it says! Store God's promises and His words of encouragement in your memory. Determine to let your thinking become as God's thinking—unlimited.

*Man's mind,
stretched to
a new idea,
never goes back
to its original
dimensions.*

**"Return to your own house, and tell
what great things God has done for you."
And he went his way and proclaimed
throughout the whole city what great
things Jesus had done for him.**

Luke 8:39 NKJV

When Michelangelo was ordered by the Pope to decorate the walls and ceiling of the Sistine Chapel, he refused. He replied that he had never done any work of that kind and that he would not undertake the job.

However, the Pope insisted and told Michelangelo that his refusal would not be accepted.

When Michelangelo came face to face with the fact that he had no alternative, he mixed his colors and went to work. And thus, what many consider to be the world's finest paintings came into existence.[8]

Few of us realize the possibilities locked up within us until necessity compels us to try something we previously thought was impossible.

Don't underestimate the impact that motivational speakers and writers can have in your life. For the most part, these men and women are very well-intentioned. They are seeking your best. They may believe in you more than you believe in you. They want to see you succeed even more than you want to succeed—they believe you can reach the top!

The first step toward changing the quality of your life is to believe that it is possible to do so. The second step is to find those who can help you get there and who will root for you along the way.

■　　■　　■

Many are satisfied to play with mud pies when they ought to be making angel food cakes. Many are building shacks when they ought to be building palaces.

His lord said unto him, Well done, good and faithful servant; thou hast been faithful over a few things, I will make thee ruler over many things: enter thou into the joy of thy lord.

Matthew 25:23 KJV

The story is told of a man who bought a ticket on a cruise ship, then took on board a supply of cheese and crackers. Throughout the voyage, he retreated to his room at mealtime to sit alone and eat his self-imposed rations. Near the end of the voyage, the captain sent for him and asked him if he was dissatisfied with the food service on the ship. The man said, "Well, the food certainly looks fine to me."

"Why then haven't we seen you in the dining room?" the captain inquired. "You once were observed sitting in your cabin eating crackers and cheese."

The man said, "I only had enough money for my steamship ticket. I didn't have anything left for meals."

To the man's great dismay the captain replied, "The price of all the meals was included in your ticket!"

This man could have been eating breakfast, brunch, lunch, high tea, dinner, and a late-night banquet on the Promenade Deck. Instead, he had settled for a diet of cheese and crackers—all because he had failed to take advantage of all that was available.

Many times we see our lives in the same way—we shortchange ourselves and fail to grab hold of all that we might have if we were only willing to see ourselves as possessing a ticket that included life's banquets.

God desires for you to prosper. His ticket to life is all-inclusive. Enjoy the feast!

■   ■   ■

Success is a journey, not a destination.

If you are pleased with me, teach me your ways so I may know you and continue to find favor with you. Remember that this nation is your people.

Exodus 33:13

*A*bout 350 years ago, a shipload of travelers landed on the northeast coast of America. In the first year they established a town. The second year they elected a town government.

The third year the town government launched a plan to build a road five miles westward into the wilderness.

In the fourth year, the people tried to impeach their town government, because they thought this plan was a waste of public funds. "Who needs to go west?" they reasoned.

These same people once had sufficient vision to sail three thousand miles across the ocean into an unknown world. They had overcome great hardships to get to America and to create a new home for themselves. Yet in just a few short years they had lost their pioneering vision.[9]

Never lose your vision for what you can become in Christ. The journey may have difficult moments, but life is just that—a journey.

Success is not a particular destination but a prevailing perspective. It is knowing you have all that you need and desire, with a joy and expectancy that God has even more in store for you.

■   ■   ■

What you get by reaching your destination isn't nearly as important as what you become by reaching that destination.

Teach me to do your will, for you are my God; may your good Spirit lead me on level ground.

Psalm 143:10

*A*n explorer named Fridtjof Nansen and a sole companion were lost in the wastelands of the Arctic. Running short on supplies as they wandered, they began to eat their sled dogs one by one, then the harnesses that their dogs had used, and finally they even consumed the whale oil they used for their lamps.

Nansen's companion gave up and lay down to die.

But Nansen would not give up. He kept telling himself over and over, "I can take one step more."

He continued to plod through the bitter cold, one step at a time, until finally, he came to the top of an ice hill and discovered an American expedition that had been sent in search of him![10]

Although he did not realize it in his state of desperation, Nansen actually used his circumstances as an opportunity to develop character. He dug deep within himself and discovered an indomitable spirit—a spirit that refused to give up. In setting out on his expedition, he had proven himself to be a dreamer and a great explorer. In surviving his expedition, he proved himself to be a conqueror and a great man.

Choose to pursue and endure. Conquer your most important territory: your inner self.

■   ■   ■

*My philosophy of life
is that if we make up
our mind what we
are going to make
of our lives, then
work hard toward
that goal, we never
lose—somehow
we win out.*

*I call heaven and earth to record
this day against you, that I have
set before you life and death, blessing
and cursing: therefore choose life,
that both thou and thy seed may live.*

Deuteronomy 30:19 *KJV*

*N*oted scientist and inventor Charles F. Kettering believed that the easiest way to overcome defeat was simply to completely ignore the possibility of failure.

He developed this theme in an address he once gave at Denison University in Granville, Ohio. He told how he had once given a tough assignment to a young researcher at the General Motors laboratory.

Just to see how the man would react to a difficult problem, Kettering did not allow him to examine notes on the subject that were on file in the GM library. These notes had been written by expert researchers, and they contained detailed statistics and reasons why the assignment that Kettering gave the young man was impossible.

The young researcher, not knowing that his effort was fruitless, went ahead with the assignment and succeeded in solving Kettering's problem![11]

Think, and then act, as if you cannot fail to achieve the goals that God has called you to pursue. With God as your Helper and Motivator, you certainly will be proven correct!

Make a decision today to succeed.

The dictionary is the only place that success comes before work.

The desire of the lazy man kills him, for his hands refuse to labor.

Proverbs 21:25 *NKJV*

*O*ne of the most amazing stories of sheer courage I have ever heard is that of Nancy Merki. At age ten, she was stricken with polio and condemned to wear heavy braces and later, to use crutches. Nancy refused to accept this as her final fate, however.

Her parents took her to Jack Cody, who was the swimming coach at an athletic club in Portland. They hoped that he might be able to help Nancy build up her leg muscles through swimming therapy. It took Cody a year to teach Nancy how to swim the length of the pool, but she was determined to succeed.

Slowly, the coach began to realize that Nancy was not only interested in swimming as a means of restoring her health and the use of her limbs, but that she had a burning desire to become a champion swimmer. Four years after her illness, she came in third place in a swim meet at Santa Barbara, California. And at age nineteen, she changed her swimming style and emerged from a national meet as champion!

When asked by President Roosevelt how she had become a champ despite her paralysis, she said simply, "Well, I guess I just kept trying, Mr. President."[12]

Keep trying—and then keep on trying. That's the number-one formula for winning.

I'm no miracle worker. I'm just a guy who rolls up his sleeves and goes to work.

And, behold, I come quickly; and my reward is with me, to give every man according as his work shall be.

Revelation 22:12 KJV

*D*uring World War II, General Douglas MacArthur once called in an Army engineer and asked him, "How long will it take to throw a bridge across this stream?"

The engineer replied crisply, "Three days, sir!"

"Good," snapped General MacArthur. "Have your draftsman make drawings right away."

Three days later the General sent for the engineer and asked how the bridge was coming along.

"It's all ready, sir! You can send the troops across right now if you don't have to wait for the drawings first. They aren't done yet."[13]

A person can sometimes spend so much time dreaming, and then planning, that he fails to actually work toward his dreams. No dream falls into a person's lap. There's always a price to be paid in terms of time, discipline, effort, and perseverance. People generally find that the harder they work, the "luckier" they become. Big "breaks" tend to happen in the wake of long hours of diligent effort.

My definition of the work ethic is this: competitive instinct applied with diligence. That's the way to get your dream off the drawing board and across the chasm to success.

■   ■   ■

I don't think anything is unrealistic if you believe you can do it. I think if you are determined enough and willing to pay the price, you can get it done.

Anyone who does not take his cross and follow me is not worthy of me.

Matthew 10:38

When eleven-year-old Jimmy learned that his home state of Ohio had no motto, he saw it as a void that should be filled. When he learned that he needed signed petitions to get state legislators to introduce a motto proposal, he shifted into high gear.

For months, most of Jimmy's spare time was spent gathering signatures door-to-door. He solicited help from his aunts who lived in other towns to help him get the necessary number of signatures. He also captured a spot on a radio show to ask for signers, and he set up a booth at a food show. He put in many long hours and much hard work!

When Jimmy finally managed to get an introduction to the governor, he explained his petition and asked, "Will you sign?" The governor did so immediately. "And what," the governor asked, "do you think would be the right motto for our state?"

Jimmy was quick to reply: "With God all things are possible."[14]

Do you have a goal today?

Do you believe that you can achieve it with God's help?

Are you doing everything you know to do to accomplish your God-given goal?

If so, I have no doubt that you are on your way to winning!

Everybody wants to go to heaven. But nobody wants to die.

**Martha saith unto him,
I know that he shall rise again
in the resurrection at the last day.**

John 11:24 *KJV*

A pastor was preaching about heaven one day, describing to the best of his ability the eternal bliss and joys that he felt sure were on the "other side." He paused for effect and asked, "How many of you here want to go to heaven?" Everyone in the sanctuary raised their hand except an eight-year-old boy on the front pew.

Looking down at him in surprise, the pastor asked, "Son, don't you want to go to heaven?"

The boy replied, "Oh yes, but I thought you were making up a load to go right now."[15]

Whether or not we will arrive in heaven one day requires more than our natural physical death. It requires that we die to the sin nature and receive God's forgiveness while we are still on this earth.

The Bible makes no promise that every person who dies will go to heaven; neither does it say that every so-called "good" person will go to heaven. Jesus said very clearly in perhaps the most famous verse of all the Bible, "For God so loved the world that He gave His only begotten Son, that whoever believes in Him should not perish but have everlasting life" (John 3:16 NKJV).

"Whoever believes in Him" is your key to entering heaven. It is your key to receiving the resurrection power that Jesus offers so freely. When you receive that power you become a true winner in life!

■ ■ ■

If you want a place in the sun, you have to put up with a few blisters.

Even youths grow tired and weary, and young men stumble and fall; but those who hope in the LORD will renew their strength. They will soar on wings like eagles; they will run and not grow weary, they will walk and not be faint.

Isaiah 40:30-31

*O*ne year, on the anniversary of Abraham Lincoln's birthday, an interesting cartoon appeared in a town newspaper. It showed a small log cabin at the base of a mountain. At the top of the mountain was the White House. The two buildings were connected by a ladder.

At the bottom of the cartoon were these words: "The ladder is still there."[16]

The ladder still exists today for you to get from where you are to where you want to be. It takes some sweat and toil, however, to climb that ladder. And sweat and toil can often be translated as smart thinking and endless hours.

The good news is that God's Word promises us that if we will keep our hope firmly connected to the Lord as we climb our individual ladders to success, He will renew our strength. In fact, according to the prophet Isaiah, we will feel as if we are flying like eagles.

What is the key to hope? I believe it lies in two things: First, reading God's Word daily as a reminder that God protects, provides for, and delivers His beloved children. He has promised His presence to us always. Second, when we begin to praise the Lord for His mighty deeds and His awesome presence with us, our hope is kindled.

Reading God's Word and giving Him praise, you can climb your ladder with joy!

■　■　■

Leadership is that certain something that is "bought with a price." Bought with a price that can be paid by anyone, anytime, anywhere.

Any of you who does not give up everything he has cannot be my disciple.

Luke 14:33

A new pastor was assigned to a congregation and after he had been there a short while, he asked his superior, "Why have you given me a church that's heavily in debt and has only a few older members?"

He was surprised when his superior replied, "We don't expect you to succeed there. We will be proud of you if you can close that church by December and do it in a harmonious way."

As the pastor prayed about this situation, he recalled that some of his classmates in seminary had been from Korea, where it was required of each seminary graduate to go into a churchless community and pioneer a church. The pastor decided, "Why not try to start a new church here?"

He encouraged the eighteen church members to invite families from the community to attend their church. When December came around, the church was out of debt and its sanctuary was almost full on Sunday mornings. Within another year, the church had more than two hundred members, and many more in attendance at its two Sunday morning services. Plans were also underway for a larger building.[17]

Don't be dismayed if you are called to lead only a few people. After all, Jesus started His ministry with only twelve disciples.

Push yourself again and again. . . . Don't give an inch until the final buzzer sounds.

Work hard at whatever you do.
Ecclesiastes 9:10 CEV

*O*g Mandino once spent a summer lecturing to writing classes held at the Arizona Biltmore Hotel in Phoenix. He opened each new course by holding up the final typeset of his book, *The Christ Commission*, and telling the eager group of would-be writers that the manuscript contained 332 pages. He then informed them that he had rewritten that particular book nine times before he was satisfied!

Mandino didn't mean that he merely changed a word or a phrase or two on a page here and there. He actually retyped the entire book nine times and made hundreds of changes each time. Furthermore, he was using an electric typewriter, not a computer! The editing process alone took nine months.

Mandino said, "The point I was hoping to make was that while they might complete a story or a novel and feel very proud of themselves and let it go at that, hoping they could sell it somewhere, the true professional, when he or she finishes a work, commences a polishing process on page one and slowly grinds through the entire book, not once but again and again until it is as good as he or she can make it."[18]

Never settle for "acceptable." Always go for "exceptional"!

Things which matter most must never be at the mercy of things which matter least.

You blind guides! You strain out a gnat but swallow a camel!

Matthew 23:24 NRSV

*T*he story is told of a man who announced to his friends and neighbors that his goal for the year was to earn a million dollars. He proceeded to develop and patent a state-of-the-art product and then travel around the country selling it, in hot pursuit of this goal.

On occasion, he would take one of his children with him on the road for a week or so. His wife complained, however, saying, "When they come back, they have stopped saying their prayers and doing their homework. A week with you is one long party. Don't take the kids if you aren't going to help them do the things they ought to be doing every day."

At the end of the year, the man announced that he had met his goal: he had made one million dollars. Shortly after that, however, he and his wife divorced, two of his children wound up on drugs, and one son nearly had a nervous breakdown. The entire family went downhill as fast as his bank account had gone uphill![19]

This man had failed to count the total cost involved in pursuing his dream.

Make certain today that your goals take your whole life into consideration, including the well-being of all whom you love. What is right for you must also be right for your family.

What good is meeting all your goals if there's no one left in your life to share them with?

■   ■   ■

You are as much a leader today as you are going to be, because the price you are paying today is determining the leader you will be tomorrow.

Jesus Christ the same yesterday, and to day, and for ever.

Hebrews 13:8 KJV

$\mathcal{A}$ customer called a computer company's service department to complain about his new printer. The service department personnel tried to help him but the customer was yelling so loudly they couldn't understand him.

When he became abusive, they passed the call to their supervisor, who also had difficulty understanding the man. The supervisor opted to make a house call to see if he could fix the problem.

When he arrived at the man's home, he found that the only thing the printer needed was a new ribbon. When the man offered to pay for his help, the supervisor replied, "I don't want any money, but I would like to say something to you. My employees provide great service and do excellent work. They are very important to me, and if you can't treat them with respect, I would prefer that you go to another store."

The man became very apologetic and agreed that his behavior had been inappropriate. Two days later, he went to the store and apologized to the two servicemen he had offended.[20]

This supervisor took a tremendous risk. Rather than blindly assuming that the customer is always right, he saw an opportunity to build employee loyalty. He was willing to pay the price of being a true leader, even if it meant losing a customer.

A good leader always makes the right decision, even when it is a hard one.

Predictability can lead to failure.

*Therefore if any man is in Christ,
he is a new creature; the old
things passed away; behold,
new things have come.*

2 Corinthians 5:17 NASB

$\mathcal{A}$ psychologist told a friend how he and his professional peers had conducted experiments with rats in mazes. He explained that they put the rat at one end of the maze and a piece of food at the other end. They then timed the rat as he bumped around the maze until he found the food. The next time the researchers put the rat in the maze, they found that he bumped less and got to the food faster. After a while, the rat became an expert at the maze—it could zip through it without any bumps and have that tidbit in his teeth within a few seconds.

Then, the psychologist explained, they took the food away. For a little while, each time the rat was put into the maze, it made a beeline for the end of the maze. It wasn't too long, however, before the rat figured out that the food wasn't going to be there so it stopped trying to get through the maze at all. The psychologist concluded: "That's the difference between rats and people. The rats know when to stop!"[21]

Unless you are willing to take new risks, set new goals for yourself, and try doing things a new way, you are going to lose your motivation for winning. Don't drive yourself into a rut. Get off the treadmill of life occasionally and ask, "Do I need a higher goal? Is there something I need to change in my life?"

Break out of the rat race! Take a risk! People will come to count on your versatility instead of your predictability!

■　■　■

*Remember,
a dead fish
can float
downstream, but
it takes a live
one to swim
upstream.*

**We do not want you to become lazy,
but to imitate those who through
faith and patience inherit
what has been promised.**

Hebrews 6:12

There once was a man who sold hot dogs by the side of the road. He was hard of hearing, so he had no radio; and he had trouble with his eyes, so he read no newspapers. He just sold good hot dogs. He put up a sign on the highway telling people how good his hot dogs were. As he stood by the side of the road, he cried, "Buy a hot dog, mister?" And people did.

The man increased his meat and bun orders. He bought a bigger stove to cook more hot dogs. Then, his son came home from college. He said, "Father, haven't you been listening to the radio or reading the papers? We're in the middle of a recession. The European situation is terrible, the Japanese situation is worse, and the situation here is worst of all."

Well, my son is in college. He reads the newspapers and listens to the radio. He must know what he's talking about, the father thought. So he decreased his meat and bun orders and took down his advertising. Sales plummeted.

"You're right," the old man said to his son a few days later. "We certainly are in the midst of a terrible recession."[22]

In spite of what others say to discourage you, keep doing what you know you have been called by God to do. Your success is His concern!

Human beings are creatures of habit. But, the only difference between a rut and a grave is its length, depth, and how long you're in it!

Therefore, since we are surrounded by such a great cloud of witnesses, let us throw off everything that hinders and the sin that so easily entangles, and let us run with perseverance the race marked out for us.

Hebrews 12:1

*T*he following statement is of unknown origin, but it nonetheless contains tremendous wisdom: "I am your constant companion. I am your greatest helper or heaviest burden. I will push you onward or drag you down to failure. I am completely at your command. Half the things you do you might just as well turn over to me and I will be able to do them quickly and correctly. I am easily managed—you must merely be firm with me. Show me exactly how you want something done and after a few lessons I will do it automatically.

"I am the servant of all great men; and alas, of all failures, as well. Those who are great, I have made great. Those who are failures, I have made failures. I am not a machine, though I work with all the precision of a machine plus the intelligence of a man. You may run me for profit or run me for ruin—it makes no difference to me. Take me, train me, be firm with me, and I will place the world at your feet. Be easy with me and I will destroy you.

"Who am I? I am habit!"[23]

To be a winner, develop and maintain godly habits. They will lead you to growth and victory in life. Ungodly habits will only lead you to destruction and demise.

Your habits can make you or break you. Choose them well!

■　　■　　■

No man is a fool to give up what he cannot keep— to gain what he cannot lose.

He that findeth his life shall lose it: and he that loseth his life for my sake shall find it.

Matthew 10:39 *KJV*

*I*n *Travels*, Michael Crichton tells about a night he spent in Malaysia. He was walking back to his cottage when a friend suddenly aimed his flashlight into the woods and said, "Mat is here."

"Mat?" Crichton asked.

"Yes," the friend said. "Mat is the Malay word for Friday, which is the day of the week this deer wandered out of the jungle and into the village. The people fed her, she stayed, and when she had offspring, some of them visited the settlement, too. That's why this village doesn't have any goats."

"What's the connection?"

His friend replied: "In every village, the Malay people like to raise goats and eat them, but once Mat arrived, the people discovered that she did not like the goats and would kick them to death. So they don't keep goats anymore."

Crichton thought to himself, "I could have thought of a dozen alternatives. An enclosure for the goats. Train Mat to tolerate goats. Raise goats at a nearby location. Discourage Mat from coming around. Still," he concluded, "where I would have struggled, the villagers simply accepted the situation and went on with life."[24]

We must each decide what is truly important to us, and let everything else fall away. This isn't accepting all situations and circumstances; it is choosing which ones to accept.

There's no reason to be the richest man in the cemetery. You can't do any business from there.

But lay up for yourselves treasures in heaven, where neither moth nor rust doth corrupt, and where thieves do not break through nor steal.

Matthew 6:20 KJV

*E*ugene Lang, a New York City philanthropist, once made a graduation speech to a sixth-grade class at Public School 121. The students there had no hope of ever going to college—indeed, they had very little hope of even graduating from high school.

At the end of his speech Lang gave them a challenge, "For any of you who graduate from high school, I will ensure that funds are available for you to go to college."

On average, only 56 percent of inner-city students graduate from high school. Of the 48 students who heard Lang that day, 44 (92 percent) graduated from high school and 42 went on to college.

It wasn't simply the offer of money that ensured these incredible results. Lang also made sure that his students were closely monitored and counseled throughout their last six years of school. Still, that one challenging goal gave these students an opportunity to dream about a future they never thought possible.[25]

Lang chose to share his wealth for the benefit of others rather than storing it up for himself. What is your motivation for becoming a winner? Set a goal that counts!

■　■　■

Half the world is on the wrong scent in the pursuit of happiness. They think it consists in having and getting. . . . On the contrary, it consists in giving, and in serving.

It is more blessed to give than to receive.
Acts 20:35

The 1983 NCAA tournament finals pitted Georgetown, coached by John Thompson, against North Carolina University. The Carolina team featured two future NBA Hall of Famers: James Worthy and Michael Jordan.

In the final minutes of the game, the lead changed hands several times. Then, with seventeen seconds left in the game, Jordan hit a jump shot that gave Carolina a 63-62 lead. The fate of the championship was in the hands of Fred Brown, Georgetown's playmaking guard. In the heat of the moment, Brown threw the ball to his opponent James Worthy, giving North Carolina the crown.

As millions gaped in disbelief and fans began to taunt Brown, Coach Thompson walked over and hugged his player. The gesture changed Brown's life, who later told a reporter, "I was really down on myself. Coach Thompson's actions made me realize that it wasn't the end of the world. Thanks to him, I'll never be the same."

The next year, Georgetown went on to win the NCAA Championship. In the waning moments of the game, with a victory assured, Coach Thompson again walked over to Fred Brown and hugged him. "We've got it, baby," he said. "Never give in or give up."[26]

When you give and serve, you will receive.

You can't build a reputation on what you are going to do.

See to it that you complete the work you have received in the Lord.

Colossians 4:17

*A*n aspiring young writer once made an appointment to interview a well-known author. The author asked him, "Why did you want to see me?" The young man responded, "Well, I'm a writer, too. I was hoping you could share with me some of your keys for success."

"What have you written?" the author asked.

"Nothing," said the young man, "at least nothing that is finished."

The writer rose from his chair and then asked, "Well, if you haven't written anything, what are you writing?"

"Well, I'm in school right now, so I'm hoping to find the time to write down some ideas."

The author began to walk toward the door, asking one final question as he showed the young man out, "Why do you call yourself a writer if you aren't writing?" When the young man gave no answer, the author said to him, "Writers write, composers compose, painters paint, and workers work. What you do to a great extent defines what you become, and, in turn, what you are gives rise to what you do. When what you do externally matches with what you are internally, greatness will not be denied!"[27]

Do what you say you want to do. Be what you claim to be. Winners win!

■ ■ ■

Even if you're on the right track, you'll get run over if you just sit there.

Every branch in Me that does not bear fruit He takes away; and every branch that bears fruit He prunes, that it may bear more fruit.

John 15:2 *NKJV*

*D*ante Gabriel Rossetti, the nineteenth-century poet and artist, was approached one autumn afternoon by an elderly man who asked Rossetti to review some of his sketches and drawings to see if they had any value. Rossetti immediately saw that the paintings were worthless.

Being a kind man, however, Rossetti tried to tell the elderly gentleman as gently as possible that his works were of little value. He was sorry, but he could not lie. The man was disappointed, yet he acted as if he had anticipated what Rossetti's evaluation would be. He apologized for taking up the artist's time, but then he asked one final favor, "Would you please look at another set of paintings that I brought along—done by a young art student?"

Rossetti's face lit up as he looked at the second set of paintings. "These are very good!" he exclaimed. "It's obvious this young artist has a great deal of skill. He should be encouraged to develop his talent." He could see that the old man was deeply moved by his words. "Who is this fine artist?" he asked. "Your son?"

"No," the old man said. "I was that artist—forty years ago. If only I had received your encouragement then, I might have grown in my talent."[28]

Grow and develop your talents. What you don't use, you lose.

■　■　■

You must get involved to have an impact. No one is impressed with the won-lost record of the referee.

But when you give a banquet, invite the poor, the crippled, the lame, the blind, and you will be blessed.

Luke 14:13-14

*M*iramar Publications has an interesting year-end reward and recognition program for its employees. The company gives $10 to each of its non-management employees and $100 to each of its managers, with instructions that each person write an anonymous note of thanks or praise to a fellow employee and enclose the cash with it.

One of the managers went to Tim Novoselski, Miramar's president, and said, "I just can't decide between two of the women I supervise—they've both done so well this year. They both deserve the money."

Novoselski half-jokingly countered, "I guess you're just going to have to take another hundred bucks out of your own pocket!" He never thought the manager would do that, but the man's eyes immediately lit up. "You're absolutely right!" he said. "That's exactly what I'm going to do!"

As you can imagine, the $100 that came from his own pocket made an even greater impression on both giver and receiver than the $100 reward from the company.[29]

A gift without your involvement is hollow. Make sure all of your giving has a big percentage of you in it.

■   ■   ■

If Columbus had had an advisory committee, he would probably still be at the dock.

By faith Noah, warned by God about events as yet unseen, respected the warning and built an ark to save his household.

Hebrews 11:7 NRSV

The story is told of two boys who went ice skating on a rural pond. One skated beyond the boundaries into the danger zone and fell through the ice. His friend, who was quite a bit younger and smaller, saw him thrash around in the icy water and then disappear under the ice. He began frantically trying to break the ice with his skates and his fists, but it wasn't working.

Then the boy spied a large tree limb at the side of the pond. He ran to it, pulled it to the spot where his friend was trapped under the ice, and amazingly, lifted it over his head and threw it, shattering a hole in the ice so that his friend could get air. Then he pulled his friend out of the icy water.

Later, as people marveled at how the smaller boy had been able to lift the huge limb and pull his larger friend from the ice, they asked, "How did you do it?" The older boy who was rescued came up with perhaps the best explanation, "He did it because there was no one there to tell him he couldn't."[30]

When you must ask for advice, always ask someone who wants you to succeed as much as you do. Otherwise, you may be better off on your own; that way no one can tell you what you can't do!

■ ■ ■

*When I've heard
all I need to
make a decision,
I don't take a
vote. I make
a decision.*

**And he saith unto them, Follow me,
and I will make you fishers of men.
And they straightway left their nets,
and followed him.**

Matthew 4:19-20 *KJV*

A game warden once noticed how a particular man seemed to consistently catch more fish than anyone else. When other fishermen would only catch three or four fish a day, this one man would come in with his boat full.

The warden finally asked the man his secret. The successful fisherman invited the game warden to accompany him and observe.

So the next morning the two men met at the dock and pushed off. When they got to the middle of the lake, the man stopped the boat, took out a stick of dynamite, lit it, and threw it into the air. The explosion rocked the lake and dead fish surfaced immediately. The man then took out a net and scooped them up.

The warden was livid. "You can't do this!" he yelled after he had recovered from the shock of this spectacle. "You'll be paying every fine in the book for this!"

The fisherman calmly set his net down, took out another stick of dynamite, lit it, and tossed it into the game warden's lap as he said, "Are you going to sit there all day complaining, or are you going to fish?"[31]

Sometimes life calls for quick decisions. Don't be afraid to make them. Ask God for His wisdom, believe you've received it, and then act on it.

When somebody says they need to refer to a committee before making a decision, you have the wrong person.

One of those days Jesus went out to a mountainside to pray, and spent the night praying to God. When morning came, he called his disciples to him and chose twelve of them.

Luke 6:12-13

*T*he story is told of a group of men who went sailing in an old boat. It was a beautiful, sunny day. The sea was calm and there was a light breeze. No one had any particular destination in mind and no one was in charge, so the boat just drifted along.

Suddenly the weather turned foul. The sky grew dark, the wind began to howl, the waves grew rough, and the rain began to fall. Before the men knew what happened, the boat had hit a rock and sprung a leak.

Although the men all knew they were in great danger, they couldn't seem to cooperate. "This is your fault!" one man yelled, to no one in particular.

Since the leak was on the starboard side of the boat, the men on the port side started insisting that the men on the starboard side repair it. But the men on the starboard side were too busy assigning blame to begin repairs.

Just before the boat sank, each man offered a plan for saving the day, but no one liked anyone else's plan enough to agree to it. So, the boat sank and they all drowned.[32]

It may be dangerous to stand up for what you think when you are in a small boat—or a small department or a small company—but it can be even more dangerous to sit and do nothing. A void in leadership will always be filled by a crisis. Step into the gap before it's too late!

■ ■ ■

If you ain't the lead dog, the scenery never changes.

Everyone who has led others to please God will shine like the stars.

Daniel 12:3 CEV

*W*hen the time came to appoint a new vice president, the president of a large company took the two top candidates to England for a series of meetings at the company's London office. Since both candidates were a close match in skill and talent, the president was hoping the trip might reveal the better of the two.

One night, the president purchased the three of them tickets to a play at a theater across town. As they waited in front of their hotel, he realized that getting a cab was going to be more difficult than he had thought.

The president enlisted the help of the doorman and sent the other two men across the street to try to hail a cab. A few minutes later, one of the men waved the others over. He had secured a ride—in a private car! As they all piled in, he explained: "I didn't think we'd find a cab in time so I flagged down cars and told people our problem until I found someone willing to give us a ride."

His method was unorthodox, but it got the job done. Resourceful and creative—the very traits the president had been looking for in a new vice president.[33]

What do you have to lose in taking an outlandish risk? If you fail, people will still call you ingenious. If you're successful, soon nobody will even remember that you were taking a risk!

Anybody who thinks they are a leader and doesn't have anybody following them is just out for a walk.

Do not think of yourself more highly than you ought.

Romans 12:3

A man who was very ambitious for honor and power once went to Rabbi Bunam and said, "My late father has appeared to me in a dream and told me that I am to be a leader of men."

Rabbi Bunam listened to the man's story in silence. A few days later, the man returned to the rabbi and said, "I have had the same dream night after night. My late father appears to me to announce that I am destined to be a leader of men."

"I understand," said the rabbi, "that you are ready to become a leader of men. Now if your father comes to you in a dream once more, tell him that you are prepared to become a leader of men, but that he should now also appear to the people you are supposed to lead to tell them."[34]

True leaders are never created by memos from headquarters, interdepartmental power struggles, or office coups. Those who foist themselves on others, flaunt their power, or demand your loyalty are not truly leaders.

A rise to genuine leadership is nearly always marked by quiet determination, humble conversation, and gentle persuasion. Always seek to earn the respect, allegiance, and admiration of others before becoming responsible for supervising them.

Everyone has an obligation as well as the privilege of leading in something. Leadership begins with a simple decision to pay the price and ends the moment you cease to pay it.

Anyone, then, who knows the good he ought to do and doesn't do it, sins.

James 4:17

A minister who wanted to build a new building began to appeal to his congregation to expand its horizons, to see a new vision.

One Sunday, he enthusiastically presented a series of high ideals and lofty goals to his congregation and then, as he reached the climax of his enthusiastic speech, he said with deep conviction, "This church must walk."

The congregation immediately responded as one, "Let 'er walk!"

Encouraged, the minister continued. "This church must run!" he exclaimed. And back came the unanimous cry, "Yes! Let 'er run!"

Extremely pleased and emotionally high, the minister proclaimed, "This church must fly!" And once again the congregation echoed his enthusiasm, "Yes, yes, let 'er fly!"

The minister quickly went on, "And that will cost money."

"Let 'er walk," came back the response.[35]

Many people are very excited about their dreams and goals—in theory. But talk to them about effort, discipline, work, and perseverance, and they cringe.

Winning always has a price—in a word, it's work. There is no substitute for sustained effort.

■   ■   ■

You can always pitch better.

Be ye therefore perfect, even as your Father which is in heaven is perfect.

Matthew 5:48 *KJV*

*I*n 1957, Don Larsen was considered the cream of the crop of baseball's major-league pitchers. Everyone expected great things from him, but he had a lackluster season and was traded twice during the next two years. Everything he did seemed to go from bad to worse. Eventually, he disappeared from the game.

Don Larsen, and everyone else, knew that he could pitch better! They weren't just hopeful—they knew he could. They had seen this six-foot-two starter for the New York Yankees take on the Brooklyn Dodgers in the fifth game of the sixty-ninth World Series, October 8, 1956.

Larsen's first pitch of that game was a strike, a good omen to Yankee fans. When the game was over, not a single Dodger batter had managed a hit, or even a walk, off Don Larsen. He had pitched the first and only no-hit, no-walk World Series game in baseball history—a perfect game!

There's a saying in baseball that's applicable to any field of endeavor: "You can't win this year's ball game on last year's record."[36]

Most people will never pitch a perfect game, but that's no reason not to set your sights on perfection. Never stop working toward being the best in your field. When you aim high, you are much more likely to do your best.

■   ■   ■

Success is to render more and better service than is expected of you.

As each one has received a special gift, employ it in serving one another, as good stewards of the manifold grace of God.

1 Peter 4:10 *NASB*

A man was having dinner with his family one night at a fine gourmet restaurant in a New York City hotel. Two of his children ordered macaroni and cheese from the children's menu. When their dinners arrived, however, they played with their food more than they ate it. When the father tasted the children's meal, he declared it to be the finest macaroni and cheese he had ever eaten. The waiter asked the children their opinion. "It's yucky!" they said candidly, "it's not Kraft."

The next evening the family again appeared at the restaurant. The waiter from the previous night spotted them and came over to the kids with an enthusiastic smile. "I was hoping you would come back," he said. "I've got Kraft for you." With that, he went to the kitchen and returned with a box of Kraft Macaroni and Cheese for their perusal.[37]

This waiter certainly went the second mile, perhaps even third mile, in service. It's no wonder that his place of employment is flourishing!

Track stars always run "through the tape." In other words, they set their sights on a point just past the finish line. The same is true for winners in every other area of life. Always seek to do more than what is required or expected, and you'll go beyond the finish line in victory!

■　■　■

You have to perform at a consistently higher level than others. That's the mark of a true professional. Professionalism has nothing to do with getting paid for your services.

But he knows the way that I take; when he has tested me, I shall come out like gold.

Job 23:10 NRSV

*M*otivational speaker Matt Weinstein guarantees his lectures: "If we do not get a standing ovation at the end of the program, we will not take a fee for our work!"

The only time Weinstein worried about not getting paid was the time he spoke to the American Public Transit Association. About ten minutes before his speech, the vice president of APTA said, "We're hoping to get a free talk out of you this morning." Weinstein replied, "You shouldn't really hope to get the talk for free, that would mean my program bombed."

The vice president replied, "Oh, you don't have to bomb. Have you taken a look at the conference program booklet?" He then showed him a copy, which read: "Due to a traumatic psychological injury incurred during his youth, Dr. Weinstein gets nervous and anxious if people in the audience clap loudly or stand abruptly at the end of his presentation. Please don't get carried away and frighten Matt. Help him out by remaining in your seats and applauding softly and graciously at the close of his presentation."

The program was a hoax, of course, and Weinstein received a spirited standing ovation at the close of his address.[38]

Regardless of the expectations of others, always expect to do your best and be your best. That's the mark of any winner!

■   ■   ■

Success lies in forming the habit of doing things that failures don't like to do.

He replied, *"My mother and brothers are those who hear God's word and put it into practice."*

Luke 8:21

*O*ne day in a Northwestern forest, a man came across a lone lumberjack. He watched for awhile as the man feverishly worked to saw down a large tree.

"What are you doing?" the man asked.

"Can't you see?" came the impatient reply from the young lumberjack. "I'm sawing down this tree."

"You look exhausted," the old-timer said. "How long have you been at this?" The young man said, "Over five hours, and I'm beat! This is very hard work."

"It looks as if your saw might be a bit dull," the older man said, not yet ready to reveal that he had more than thirty years of experience as a lumberjack.

"It probably is," he said. "I've been sawing for hours."

"Why don't you take a break for a few minutes and sharpen that saw?" the old lumberjack suggested. "I'm sure your job would go a lot faster." The young man said, "I don't like to sharpen. And right now I don't have time to sharpen. I'm too busy sawing!"[39]

Whatever your job in life, you must be willing to do all of the tasks involved, including those you don't like. Remember the saying, "An ounce of prevention is worth a pound of cure"? Well, an ounce of preparation, however unpleasant, is worth a ton of work!

■   ■   ■

The world is full of willing people, some willing to work, the others willing to let them.

Then saith he unto his disciples, The harvest truly is plenteous, but the labourers are few.

Matthew 9:37 KJV

A very successful man well-known for his quick wit was being interviewed for a magazine article. He was asked to give his opinion of why he had been so successful. The interviewer attempted to steer his comments by saying, "Most of the men I've spoken to so far attribute their success to hard work."

The man smiled and said, "I guess that applies to me, too. I was brought up on a farm. One very hot day I was distributing and packing down the hay which a stacker was constantly dumping on top of me. By noon I was completely exhausted. That afternoon I left the farm, never to return, and I haven't done a day of hard work since."[40]

Although this famous lawyer, Clarence Seward Darrow, may not have engaged in hard physical labor after that day on the farm, he certainly worked hard at his profession. He was renowned for his labor litigation and murder cases.

The difference between a winner and a loser can often be summed up in one word: effort. Losers try to get by on their charm and luck. Winners are willing to put in the time necessary to do research, learn new skills, and hone their talents.

Are you making an effort?

■   ■   ■

The average person puts only 25 percent of his energy and ability into his work. The world . . . stands on its head . . . for those few and far between souls who devote 100 percent.

You need to persevere so that when you have done the will of God, you will receive what he has promised.

Hebrews 10:36

*O*ne day the president of a large company was walking the halls of his building and stopping into office after office. An eager assistant accompanied him, clipboard in hand, to make notes of the president's impressions, orders he might give, or changes he might want to make. When the president came to a large corner office where the occupant was sitting back in his chair with his feet on his desk, staring out the window, he said to his assistant, "Just look at him."

The assistant, thinking the president was upset by this sight of an employee so obviously wasting time said, "It's a shame, sir. He's wasting your money."

"To the contrary," the president said. "That man once had an idea that saved us millions of dollars. At the time, I believe his feet were planted right where they are now. I am more than willing to pay him to come up with more such ideas!"

Hoping to make amends, the assistant sheepishly suggested, "Shall I order him a larger window, sir?"[41]

Give your best creative energy to any project you undertake. Giving 100 percent doesn't always mean making a big commotion; it often means quieting yourself and giving 100 percent of your concentration.

The price [of leadership]: loneliness, weariness, abandonment, vision.

Then he returned to the three disciples and found them asleep. "Peter," he called, "couldn't you even stay awake with me one hour?"

Matthew 26:40 TLB

A wise and beloved shah once ruled the land of Persia. He cared about his people deeply and wanted only the best for them. With this intent, he periodically disguised himself and wandered through the streets in an effort to see life from the perspective of his subjects.

One day he disguised himself and went to the public baths. The water for the baths was heated by a furnace in the cellar, where one man was responsible for maintaining the water's temperature. The shah made his way to the basement to visit with the man who tended the fire. They shared a meal together and the shah befriended him.

Day after day, week after week, the shah went to visit the fire-tender. The fire-tender grew very fond of his visitor, because no other person had ever come down to where he was or showed such concern for him.

Finally, the day came when the shah revealed his true identity. It was a risky move, since he feared the man might ask him for special favors. Instead, the fire-tender looked into the shah's eyes and said, "On other people you might bestow rich gifts, but to me you have given the best gift of all. You have given yourself."[42]

Give the gift of your friendship. It is the greatest gift you will ever give to those you lead—or follow.

■ ■ ■

Champions . . . trust God while others ask for answers. They step forward while everyone else prays for volunteers.

Mordecai the Jew was second in rank to King Xerxes, preeminent among the Jews, and held in high esteem by his many fellow Jews, because he worked for the good of his people and spoke up for the welfare of all the Jews.

Esther 10:3

$\mathcal{W}$alking down a city street in the dead of winter, a young priest passed a small boy—homeless and skinny, his clothing threadbare. He stood for a moment and watched as the boy huddled over a street grate, trying to absorb the heat from the subway tunnel below.

"God!" the priest exclaimed in his frustration at the sight of the shivering child. "Why do You allow this? Why don't You do something? Don't You care?"

He heard the Lord's voice say to his spirit, "I do care, and I have done something about it. I created you and sent you here."[43]

In the Bible, Nehemiah was a man who recognized that God had created him for a special task. When Nehemiah heard that Jerusalem was in ruins, his first response was to fast and pray. His second response was to be quick to answer the king who questioned his sad countenance, "I ask that you send me to Judah, to the city of my fathers' tombs, that I may rebuild it" (Nehemiah 2:5 NKJV). His third response was to go and build!

Fifty-two days after Nehemiah arrived in Jerusalem, a new wall and new gates had been built and the city was secure.

Don't question the problem or why it's there. Question what you might do to bring about an answer!

When you're interested in something, you do it only when it's convenient. When you're committed to something, you accept no excuses, only results.

But your hearts must be fully committed to the LORD our God, to live by his decrees and obey his commands.

1 Kings 8:61

When Nikolay Avilov of the USSR set a world record of 8,454 points in the decathlon at the 1972 Olympics, Bruce Jenner watched his medal ceremony. He has said, "I had what you might call a life-altering experience. I saw myself standing on that victory platform at the 1976 Olympic Games. Suddenly, I knew if I could do the work, I could win the Gold."

Jenner returned to his dorm room about 11 p.m. that night, but he couldn't sleep. The thought kept coming to him, "If you're going to dedicate every second to winning the decathlon, what are you doing wasting your time in bed?" So he got up and went for a jog.

For the next four years, Jenner gave himself completely to his goal. Every decision he made was weighed against the question, "Will it increase my chances for winning the gold medal at the 1976 Olympic Games?" For Jenner, this wasn't a business decision. He was strictly an amateur—one man going up against history in a contest that generally earned its winner the title of World's Greatest Athlete.

In 1976, his moment came! He not only won the Gold, but set a new world record—8,634 points.[44]

Are you fully committed to realizing your dreams? Make every decision based upon that commitment.

■   ■   ■

*It is better
to do nothing
at all than to do
something badly.*

**For they sow the wind, and
they reap the whirlwind.**

Hosea 8:7 *NASB*

*O*ne Thanksgiving, a young man and his college roommate decided that if they couldn't go home for the holiday, they'd invite a group of friends to join them at their apartment for a home-cooked feast. As the day approached, the two made their shopping list and began preparations. The man suspected they might be in trouble when he discovered that his roommate didn't even know how to use an electric can opener. The problem was even greater, however, when he took on the challenge of the turkey.

First, he failed to remove the bag of giblets from the bird's cavity. Next, he decided to rub oil on the skin just as his mother had done. The only oil he had, however, was 3-in-1 oil. Fortunately, there wasn't much left in the can. When he discovered how long it took to roast a turkey and realized he hadn't even preheated the oven, he set it to its highest setting and placed the turkey directly on the metal rack in the oven—no roasting pan.

Then, he went out to pick up the friends they had invited. He returned to find firemen emerging from his apartment, which was belching black smoke, carrying a charred turkey.

In the end, the young man drove his roommate and their guests to a local cafeteria.[45]

There are times to try something new on your own and there are times to let someone with experience do it. Winners know the difference.

■　■　■

Success in life comes not from holding a good hand, but from playing a poor hand well.

Most gladly, therefore, I will rather boast about my weaknesses, that the power of Christ may dwell in me.

2 Corinthians 12:9 NASB

*O*bservers of the 1896 presidential election saw a great mismatch. William McKinley, the underdog, was the down-home, folksy governor from Ohio. The favorite was the great, stem-winding orator, Congressman William Jennings Bryant.

McKinley knew his strengths, however. He was pure heartland, the stable guy next door, more at home on his front porch than the campaign trail. He also knew his weaknesses: lack of personal charisma and virtually no oratorical skill. Given this mix, McKinley wisely decided not to go out on the campaign trail. He chose to stay at home and conduct the first "front porch campaign" in American history. He invited America to visit him one by one. And America came.

One man who went to see McKinley was journalist George Stevens. He later wrote, "I rang and walked in. Mr. McKinley was sitting in a rocking chair not ten feet from the door. He is gifted with a kindly courtesy that is plainly genuine and completely winning." And win he did. McKinley became the twenty-fifth president of the United States.[46]

Ask God to help you identify and then build on your strengths. And then, ask Him to help you find able assistants and friends who can compensate for your weaknesses.

■   ■   ■

There is more credit and satisfaction in being a first-rate truck driver than a tenth-rate executive.

But you, be sober in all things, endure hardship . . . fulfill your ministry.

2 Timothy 4:5 *NASB*

A customer service consultant once told a large group of front-line service people who worked for a grocery chain: "Each of you should put your own signature on your job. What could you do that is uniquely you, that tells your customers they are important?" Three weeks later she heard from a bagger named Johnny, a young man with Down's syndrome.

He said, "The night after I heard you speak to us, my parents and I talked about what I could do special for my customers. I've collected good quotations over the years, and we decided I would give them to the people I serve at the store."

Johnny went on to tell how he had typed his list of quotes on the family computer, made 150 copies of each, and then cut them out individually and folded them. Each day, he chose one of his quotes and as he finished bagging each customer's groceries, he said, "I'm putting my quote for the day in your bag. I hope it makes your day brighter." The store manager soon noted that every time he looked, all the customers were in Johnny's aisle![47]

Regardless of the position you hold today, ask God to help you be the best you can be, and to reflect His character in all you do and say. There's no one else who can do what you do like you!

■   ■   ■

*The life
which is
unexamined
is not worth
living.*

**Test yourselves and find out if you
really are true to your faith.**
2 Corinthians 13:5 CEV

*T*he story is told of a family who allowed their home to become dirty and run down, inside and out. Neighbors pleaded with the family to clean up their property, but to no avail.

One autumn day a friend of this family gave them a flower bulb and asked them to plant it under their window. It was a gesture of friendship, so the family did as the friend asked. The next spring, a little green shoot pushed its way to the surface and soon a yellow flower unfolded. As the family sat in their front room, the wife said, "That flower is so beautiful, I think I'll clean the window so we can get a better look at it."

After she had washed the windows, she noticed her curtains looked drab, so she washed them too. Her husband, moved by the contrast between the curtains and the room, decided to repaint the room. Then, noting the contrast between the inside of the house and outside, he decided to paint the outside of the house. Then, once the house was repainted, the yard naturally had to be spruced up so as not to detract from the rest of the house![48]

Few of us are able to see the complex picture of our lives all at once, but if we start by examining just one area of our life, we can begin to make small improvements that eventually will bring about a better whole!

Ask God to reveal to you the area of your life that you need to reexamine today.

■   ■   ■

What lies behind us and what lies before us are small matters compared to what lies within us.

Greater is he that is in you, than he that is in the world.

1 John 4:4 KJV

A king once hired a carpenter to build houses for his subjects. The man's work pleased both the king and the people who lived in the houses. Therefore, the carpenter soon became wealthy from the king's generous fees.

One day the carpenter reasoned, "The king is paying me handsomely, yet I am the only one who knows the quality of materials I use and the extra effort I take. From now on, I'll make the outside of the houses beautiful, but on the inside, I'll use materials that don't cost as much."

That is precisely what he did. And as he had anticipated, nobody knew that he was cutting corners and he became even more wealthy.

Then the day came when the king asked the carpenter to build the finest house he had ever built. "Spare no expense," the king said. The carpenter was overjoyed. Here was a chance to make even more profit! He used second-rate materials and sloppy workmanship. When he was finished, the king paid him as if he had done a first-rate job, and then said, "And now, I give this house to you as a gift for all you have done!"[49]

The carpenter had to live in his shabbily-constructed home for the rest of his life.

Take care in choosing what materials go into the building of your life. You will have to live with your choices for all eternity.

The Lord works from the inside out. The world works from the outside in. The world would shape human behavior, but Christ can change human nature.

Even though our outer nature is wasting away, our inner nature is being renewed day by day.
2 Corinthians 4:16 NRSV

When Rabbi Wayne Dosick was a boy, new brick homes were being built in his Chicago neighborhood. Every day after the workmen left, the kids in his neighborhood played in the excavations. One day a gigantic stack of bright red bricks arrived at the building site. Dosick just had to have one, and so did all the other children.

It never occurred to Dosick that taking a brick might be a problem. After all, there were thousands of them. His parents, however, had a different opinion.

"It's stealing," his father said. His mother added, "First thing tomorrow morning, before you go to school, you take that brick back, give it to the workman, and apologize for taking his brick."

Dosick protested, "It's only one brick."

"But how many of you took only one brick?" his father asked. He admitted that ten or twelve kids had each taken a brick. "Now it's not just one brick, but ten or twelve. . . . What if a hundred thousand kids took just one brick." Suddenly Dosick saw the big picture. If everyone stole only one brick, there would be no houses.[50]

One small sin may seem insignificant, but it infects the whole of your soul. Face up to your sin today and ask God to forgive you and help you to change your ways. Winning over sin is one of the sweetest victories in life.

■　■　■

We make a living by what we get. But we make a life by what we give.

Freely ye have received, freely give.
Matthew 10:8 KJV

V. P. Menon was a significant political figure in India during its struggle for independence from Britain after World War II. He had experienced a meteoric rise in life. The eldest son of twelve children, he quit school at thirteen and worked as a laborer, coal miner, factory hand, merchant, and schoolteacher. In each position, he had built a reputation as a man of integrity.

When Menon arrived in Delhi to seek his first government job, all of his possessions—including his money and ID—were stolen at the railroad station. In desperation he turned to an elderly Sikh, explained his troubles, and asked for a temporary loan of fifteen rupees to tide him over until he could get work. The Sikh gave him the money. When Menon asked for his address so that he could repay him, the Sikh said that Menon owed the debt to any stranger who came to him in need, as long as he lived. The help came from a stranger, and it was to be repaid to a stranger.

Menon never forgot. The day before he died, his last conscious act was to give fifteen rupees to a beggar who came to his home asking for money to buy new sandals for his sore-covered feet.[51]

Give what you can to as many as you can as often as you can. After all, God gave to you all that you have!

To be a man is to matter to someone outside yourself, or to some calling or cause bigger than yourself.

But you are a chosen race, a royal priesthood, a holy nation, a people for God's own possession.

1 Peter 2:9 *NASB*

*O*ne night in 1979, Vietnam veteran Jan Scruggs went to see the movie *The Deer Hunter*. The next day, he decided that he would build a memorial to honor those who had died in Vietnam. He later held a press conference to announce the formation of the Vietnam Veterans' Memorial Fund and immediately received praise from veterans and skepticism from just about everyone else.

Still, Scruggs was a man with a mission. He was determined that the memorial—as yet neither funded nor designed—would be dedicated three years later on November 13, Veteran's Day, 1982.

It was.

Scruggs no doubt felt he had to fight the war all over again before the monument became a reality. There were fights over where to locate the memorial and squabbles over the design. Construction permits were withheld. But in the end, the Veterans Wall, with its more than 58,000 engraved names, was built on the Mall between the Washington and Lincoln memorials in Washington, DC.[52]

Scruggs was dedicated to a cause bigger than himself. Are you? Does your concern for others compel you to want to serve them and honor them? Ask God to give you a true mission for your life.

When you are making a success of something, it's not work. It's a way of life. You enjoy yourself because you are making your contribution to the world.

Your love has given me great joy and encouragement, because you, brother, have refreshed the hearts of the saints.

Philemon 7

*E*ach year in professional sports, millions of dollars are spent on individual athletes. Team owners and managers are eager to do everything possible to protect their investments, and contracts routinely prohibit players from risking injury in off-season recreational activities. Even touch football or pick-up basketball games are forbidden.

Michael Jordan, arguably the greatest basketball player of all time, has insisted however, on having a "love of the game" clause in his contract. It allows him to participate in informal, playground competitions whenever and wherever he wants.[53]

Love of the game! Michael Jordan has been playing basketball virtually all his life. He plays nearly a hundred games a year at the most intense level of professional competition. He earns millions of dollars for his efforts. Basketball is his job, and yet he still wants to be able to go and play basketball whenever, wherever he wants, for the love of the game. Is it any wonder he is such a big winner?

Anytime that you start thinking of work as something that you have to do, as opposed to something that you get to do, it's time to reevaluate. If necessary, ask God to rekindle your dream, refocus your efforts, or redirect your course in life. Do it "for the love of your work."

Effective managers live in the present— but concentrate on the future.

Things that are seen don't last forever, but things that are not seen are eternal. That's why we keep our minds on the things that cannot be seen.

2 Corinthians 4:18 *CEV*

An executive once went to China to meet with a major silk manufacturer. He arrived at the factory at 1:30 in the afternoon and found the place strangely quiet. His driver escorted him inside and the first person he saw was the receptionist—stretched out on a mat on the floor, asleep!

"Ah," the driver said, "sleep time."

The driver led the executive down a hall past dozens of offices, design rooms, and tea lounges—all with sleeping workers. When they reached the chairman's office he could see through the half-opened door that the chairman was sacked out on a sofa.

The driver whispered, "You wait here. Sleep time almost over."

The executive sat down on a soft silk chair and within minutes, he too drifted to sleep. Precisely at two o'clock, however, he awakened to the sound of a ringing bell. Within three minutes, he and the chairman were talking as if it was nine o'clock in the morning. The executive said, "I have never seen a workplace so bustling. Everyone was on his toes. Everyone was concentrating."[54]

This factory had obviously discovered that meeting present individual needs was a means to a brighter corporate future.

Ask God for those things that will not only improve your life today but also prepare you for eternity!

■   ■   ■

Nobody gets to live life backward. Look ahead— that's where your future is.

I run toward the goal, so that I can win the prize of being called to heaven. This is the prize that God offers because of what Christ Jesus has done.

Philippians 3:14 CEV

*A*lbert Dunlap, who is an expert at turning around sick companies, once worked with executives at Scott Paper. At the time he arrived, the company had lost $277 million the previous year, its stock was stagnant, and they had no marketing strategy. Worst of all, Dunlap found that neither managers nor employees believed the decline could be stopped.

In his first week at Scott Paper, Dunlap called a meeting of all the senior managers. He asked each person to stand and tell what he or she was going to do for the company. One man began to relate what he had done for the company over the years. Dunlap interrupted, "I don't care what you have done. I want to know what you are going to do. Now and in the future!"

The man was stunned. Needless to say, at every meeting thereafter, each person was prepared to say what he or she was going to do to help the company.[55]

That one small change in focus caused a huge change in attitude that infused the company with new energy. By December 1995, Scott was virtually debt-free and the value of its stock had improved by more than 200 percent!

Often we approach God with a "what can You do for me today?" attitude. Today, make your prayer, "Lord, here's what I desire to do for You and Your Kingdom!"

■   ■   ■

You can't have a better tomorrow if you are thinking about yesterday all the time.

Forget the former things; do not dwell on the past.

Isaiah 43:18

A number of years ago on the *Today* show, Willard Scott interviewed a Mr. Smith, who was celebrating his 102nd birthday. Mr. Smith had brought along his potted plants, which he proudly called his "upstarts." Willard became a little frustrated with Mr. Smith, who directed his attention to his chrysanthemums and orchids more than to Willard and the program.

Willard finally asked, "But, Mr. Smith, we'd all like to know to what you attribute your long life."

Mr. Smith, not the least bit senile, continued to show off his flowers, lovingly touching them and spraying them with water. "This little lovely won't bloom for another two years," he chuckled.

Willard persisted. "What's your secret for living so long and staying so alive, Mr. Smith?"

"Who would take care of these beautiful flowers?" Mr. Smith replied.[56]

Mr. Smith obviously had a purpose in life that kept him focused on the present and the future, not the past.

Make spending eternity with God the overriding perspective of your life. Then everything else will fall into place.

Do not judge, and you will never be mistaken.

He who answers a matter
before he hears it,
It is folly and shame to him.

Proverbs 18:13 NKJV

*W*hen word began to spread that the Carlisle Indians had an outstanding track team, the coach of the powerful Lafayette College team, Harold Anson Bruce, invited "Pop" Warner's athletes to a dual meet. The meet was widely publicized and quickly sold out.

Bruce was dismayed, however, when he went to greet the visitors and saw only a few young men get off the train with Pop Warner. "Where are your Indians?" Bruce demanded.

"I've got enough," Warner answered.

"How many?" asked Bruce. "Five," said Warner.

"But Pop," Bruce said, "I've got a team of forty-six. It's an eleven-event program. This is a disaster. You haven't a chance." Warner simply replied, "Wanna bet?"

What Bruce didn't know was that Jim Thorpe—who went on to decathlon and pentathlon fame in the 1912 Olympics—was a Carlisle Indian. Thorpe won the high jump, the broad jump, the pole vault, the shot put, and the low hurdles. He came in second in the 100-meter dash. Two others ran first and second in the half-mile, the mile, and the two-mile events, and another won the quarter-mile. The fifth player won the high hurdles. In the end, Carlisle won 71-31.[57]

Harold Bruce's assessment about the Indians may have seemed logical based on what he saw. But it was what he couldn't see on the surface—the inner strength of these five athletes—that made all the difference and led the Carlisle Indians to an amazing victory.

By going beyond the surface and getting the "inside" story, winners gain the insight to believe the best of others.

The trouble with most of us is that we would rather be ruined by praise than saved by criticism.

*Those whom I love
I rebuke and discipline.*
Revelation 3:19

*I*n *From Bad Beginnings to Happy Endings*, Ed Young recalls a family who were members of a church he once pastored. Two of the family's grown sons—in their late twenties—still lived in a converted attic room in their parents' home. They both worked at the local mill where their father worked.

On weekends, the boys followed the practice of many of the mill workers—they went to the local honky tonk, got drunk, and occasionally wound up in jail. Every time this happened, their father bailed them out, because he was a "good, respectable" man. And it seemed to him to be the fatherly thing to do.

One night, Young received the call he had always feared. The boys had been out drinking. On their way home, they had engaged in a heated argument. One son had killed the other.

The boys' mother went to Young after the funeral service and asked, "Oh pastor, where did we go wrong?" Young comforted her, but he could not answer her question. She was asking it two decades too late.[58]

We are "grown up" when we discipline ourselves and assume discipline for those for whom we are responsible before God. Leadership not only includes love and mercy, but also the willingness to take a strong stand for what is right.

Winners know how to give and receive loving criticism.

Don't be afraid of shortcomings, because they are what will make you better. Stay on the right track, continue to pray and things will work out for you.

And we know that God causes all things to work together for good to those who love God, to those who are called according to His purpose.

Romans 8:28 *NASB*

A man once made an appointment with his wise and good old rabbi. Wringing his hands, the troubled man confessed, "Rabbi, I'm a failure. More than half the time I do not succeed in doing what I must do. Please say something wise to help me."

The rabbi pondered the situation for a moment and then said, "My son, go look on page 930 of *The New York Times Almanac* for the year 1970, and you will find peace of mind."

The man left and did what the rabbi had advised. On that page he discovered a listing of the lifetime batting averages of some of the country's greatest baseball players. Ty Cobb, the supreme slugger, had a lifetime average of only .367.

The man was puzzled. He returned to his rabbi and said, "Ty Cobb, .367, that's it?" The rabbi said, "Right. Ty Cobb, .367. You came to me complaining that you feel wretched because you only succeed in doing what you must do half of the time. Cobb would have been thrilled with that percentage!"[59]

Our failures do not define us, especially in God's eyes. We are defined by our willingness to give our failures to God and trust Him to use them for our eternal good. Never allow yourself to become discouraged. Remember, God works everything out for your good when you follow Him!

A man who trims himself to suit everybody will soon whittle himself away.

Saul said to Samuel, "I have sinned; for I have transgressed the commandment of the LORD and your words, because I feared the people and obeyed their voice."

1 Samuel 15:24 NRSV

A dim-witted man once bought a new suit from a lazy tailor. The first day that he wore his suit, a friend pointed out to him that the right sleeve was far too short. The dim-witted man went back to the lazy tailor, who said, "Oh, it doesn't need alteration. Just raise your right shoulder, then pull and hold the sleeve with your left hand." The dim-witted man did as he was told, but it caused him to hunch over and walk with a lurch.

As he left the tailor's shop, he met another friend. "How do you like my suit?" he asked. "Nice," the friend replied, "but your left pants leg seems awfully short." So the dim-witted man headed back into the tailor shop.

"Oh, that's because when you lean over to hold up your right sleeve, you pull up your left pants leg. Just lift your left leg until your cuff reaches the top of your shoe."

The man left the tailor shop and hobbled down the street toward his office. As he passed in front of two men dining at a sidewalk cafe, one of them said to the other, "Poor man, I wonder what happened to him?" The other replied, "I can't begin to guess, but given the way he has to walk, isn't it amazing how well his suit fits?"[60]

Whose expectations are you attempting to live up to today? The only opinion that really counts is God's.

I don't know the key to success, but the key to failure is trying to please everybody.

Am I now trying to win the approval of men, or of God?

Galatians 1:10

*I*n *Everyone's a Coach*, Ken Blanchard tells about his first teaching experience when he was fresh out of graduate school. He was hired as administrative assistant to the dean of a business school, but his duties included teaching a management class.

The first day of class, he told the students, "I'm Ken Blanchard, your teacher for this course. Call me Ken. We're going to teach this course together. Don't worry about grades—you'll have to work at it to make less than an A."

He then said, "If you'd rather spend time elsewhere where you have more interest, by all means do it. . . . At the end of the course, I'll give you an exam based on the book. Your performance on this test will constitute your grade."

He then suggested that those who just wanted to take the exam at the course end could leave. Within a couple of minutes, the size of his class went from a hundred students to only eight![61]

In his great desire to be liked by his students, Blanchard had acted in a way that neither earned their respect, nor their friendship.

Remember, the world likes winners. Choose to be admired and respected rather than just liked.

■   ■   ■

Often, we avoid situations and people where the risks of failure and rejection are high. We need to . . . live for Christ rather than for the approval of other people.

So do not be ashamed to testify about our Lord.
2 Timothy 1:8

*I*n 1992 and 1993, Richard Capen served as the US Ambassador to Spain. He writes in *Finish Strong*: "In Spanish, the ambassador and his wife are referred to as los embajadores, suggesting a team. We liked that inference. But not everything we did pleased everyone. At the embassy, for example, Joan started each meal with a blessing, whether we were alone in our small, private dining room on the second floor or seated with seventy-five others in the formal first-floor dining room. As we bowed our heads around the table, we held hands as was our custom at home. We wanted to be authentic, and prayer was a very important part of our authenticity.

"Soon the word leaked out and *Tiempo*, one of Spain's leading weekly newsmagazines, ran a feature story about our tradition. The article was headlined 'The Praying Ambassador.' The editors . . . accused me of trying to remake Spain. . . . Our simple effort to thank God for His many blessings was seen as an attempt to reunite church and state. Today, that magazine article is framed in my California office as a badge of honor."[62]

True inner peace comes in part from being true to your beliefs. What small change can you make today to regain your inner peace and renew your commitment to live for Christ?

If you don't know where you are going, you will probably wind up somewhere else.

But Moses said [to Hobab], **"Please do not leave us. You know where we should camp in the desert, and you can be our eyes."**

Numbers 10:31

A cardiologist once hired a consultant to help him recruit a general practitioner for his practice. He had read that the trend was moving toward increased funding for general practitioners and away from specialists, so he decided that he should have a good GP on his staff.

The consultant began her work by meeting with the staff and asking, "Who are your patients? How do they become your patients?" She discovered that 87 percent of the cardiologist's practice came from referrals made by local general practitioners. Armed with this fact, she asked him, "Do you really want to replace 87 percent of your business the day you hire your own GP?" The cardiologist turned pale at the thought.[63]

This man, a brilliant physician, was on the brink of making a mistake that could have cost him hundreds of thousands of dollars, because he based a business decision on what he had read in a couple of magazine articles rather than on solid research of his clientele.

The best way to get the best advice that you will need for all of life, and on into eternity, is to read the Bible daily. Base your life on solid research of the Truth. God always knows where you're going!

■ ■ ■

The greater thing in this world is not so much where we stand as in what direction we are going.

By faith Abraham obeyed when he was called to go out to the place which he would receive as an inheritance. And he went out, not knowing where he was going.

Hebrews 11:8 *NKJV*

For years, a man routinely drove through one of the seventeen tollbooths on the San Francisco-Oakland Bay Bridge without incident. Then one day he pulled up to a tollbooth and it was vibrating like a bass drum. He looked around. No other drivers had their windows open. There was no boom box on the sidewalk. The sound was coming from the booth. When he looked in he saw the attendant dancing!

"What are you doing?" the man asked as he paid his toll and put out a hand to receive his change.

"I'm having a party!" said the attendant.

The man pointed to the other sixteen attendants with their stern expressions. "Your friends don't seem to be," he noted.

"No," the attendant smiled, "they're in vertical coffins. At eight-thirty every morning, live people get in. Then they die for eight hours. At four-thirty, like Lazarus from the dead, they reemerge and go home."

The attendant then pointed to the administration building by the side of the road. "I'm going to be a dancer someday," he said. "My bosses are paying for my training."[64]

One out of seventeen had found a way to live and work at the same time!

Are you standing still, or are you going someplace today? God has called you to go forward, so start moving!

■　　■　　■

Many well-meaning but ineffective managers are working . . . without the slightest idea of what direction they are moving. Most organizations are overmanaged and underled.

Those who guide this people mislead them, and those who are guided are led astray.

Isaiah 9:16

*I*n *Empires of the Mind*, Denis Waitley tells about his efforts to keep a speaking engagement he had in Toronto. On the day of the event, Waitley awoke to find that a snowstorm had caused all flights in the city where he was staying to be canceled. He knew that the hall in Toronto had already been hired and a large audience was expected. No excuse would be good enough for not showing up!

Determined to get to Toronto, Dennis chartered a small plane with a brave pilot. After risking his life and paying $5,000 for a turbulent ride, he landed in Toronto and hailed a cab. He gave the driver the address of the hotel where he was scheduled to speak and told him he needed to be there in a hurry. The driver tore through the city, only to come face to face with a problem. No convention had been booked at the hotel on his itinerary, because the hotel had been torn down six months earlier! Somehow his office had failed to receive notice that the convention had been moved to Vancouver.

The taxi driver, upon learning of the magnitude of the error, asked as he drove Waitley back to the airport, "Shouldn't you call your wife before you fly home? Maybe she moved too."[65]

Make sure that you are going where you truly want to go and where God is truly leading you to go.

■   ■   ■

I believe the first test of a truly great man is humility.

Do nothing from selfish ambition or conceit, but in humility regard others as better than yourselves.

Philippians 2:3 *NRSV*

*K*ing Oswin, ruler of the former British province of Deira, once gave Bishop Aidan a fine horse. Soon afterward, Bishop Aidan met a beggar who asked him for alms. The bishop at once dismounted and gave the man his newly acquired horse, complete with its costly trappings.

When this charitable deed came to the king's attention, he railed at the bishop: "Why did you give away the horse that we specially chose for your personal use when we knew that you had need of one for your journeys? We have many less valuable horses that would have been suitable for beggars!"

Bishop Aidan replied, "Is this foal of a mare more valuable to you than a child of God?" The king immediately felt deeply convicted and fell at Bishop Aidan's feet, begging both his forgiveness and God's.

Equally moved, the bishop urged the king to rise and go to his dinner and be merry. He said as the king left his presence: "I know that the king will not live long, for I have never seen a king so humble." Shortly thereafter, Oswin was killed.[66]

Those who are willing to admit their errors and bow humbly before others to ask forgiveness are those who will one day be raised up to stand before God's throne.

Success in marriage consists not only in finding the right mate, but also in being the right mate.

Nevertheless let each individual among you also love his own wife even as himself; and let the wife see to it that she respect her husband.

Ephesians 5:33 *NASB*

ormer President Jimmy Carter, writing in *Living Faith*, tells about a gift he once gave to his wife Rosalynn: "I was very busy at the time, putting the final touches on a book. I went into my study early one morning, turned on my computer, and there it was: August 18, her birthday, and I hadn't gotten her a present! Rosalynn was still in bed, so I started wondering what I could give her that I didn't have to go down to my cousin Hugh's antique store to buy."

Carter began to reflect on his relationship with Rosalynn and specifically on one of the biggest problems in their marriage.

All of his life, Carter had always shown up early for appointments. He had no patience for those who kept him waiting. Although Rosalynn was never more than two or three minutes "late," her tardiness was irritating to him, and his irritation was in turn irritating to her.

Then it dawned on him. He wrote a note to her, which said, "Rosalynn, I promise you that for the rest of our marriage, I will never make an unfavorable remark about tardiness."

He signed it and gave it to her for a present. She agrees —it was the best birthday present he ever gave her.[67]

When you respect your spouse, you can truly respect yourself.

If America is going to survive . . . it will be because husbands and fathers again place their families at the highest level on their system of priorities.

For you know that we dealt with each of you as a father deals with his own children, encouraging, comforting and urging you to live lives worthy of God.

1 Thessalonians 2:11-12

*E*ven though the basketball game was forty years ago, Ray Meyer, former coach of DePaul University, still remembers coaching his team against Adolph Rupp of the famous Kentucky Wildcats. The game was the first major potential victory for the young coach, against one of the top teams in the nation.

With his wife, Marge, in the stands, Meyer paced the floor shouting plays. The score was tied with only a few seconds left. DePaul had the ball, but then a Kentucky player stole it and scored a basket. Ouch.

Meyer and his players were very disappointed. Still, Meyer did his best to console the young players and speak positively to reporters. As he drove home, he told himself he had handled the loss as well as could be expected.

Well, almost. At midnight, the phone rang. It was Marge—he had left her at the stadium.

Meyer decided that was no way to live. When his son became coach at DePaul, Meyer said to him: "Enjoy life. Hug your wife. Cherish your son. Quit thinking the world revolves around DePaul basketball. Ten years from now, who will care? Do this and sleep will come easier and the craving for antacid tablets will lessen."[68]

Jesus taught that seeking God's Kingdom must always be our first priority. Your family should always be a close second!

■ ■ ■

There are no little things.

*Therefore, when I was planning this,
did I do it lightly?*

2 Corinthians 1:17 NKJV

A man once discovered that an important package had been sent to his home address rather than his office, so he waited at home for the delivery. As the day wore on, he became more and more frustrated. Finally his wife suggested he take their dog, Grover, for a walk.

As the man headed outside with his dog, the UPS truck pulled up. The executive was ready to unload his pent-up anger on the driver but before he could, the driver reached into his pocket, pulled out a dog biscuit, and stuffed it into Grover's drooling mouth.

"Good-looking pup, aren't you?" he said to the dog. "What's his name?" he asked the man.

"It's Grover," replied the executive. "He's lucky to have a master like you," the driver said. "You are no doubt a busy man, but you still take the time to take Grover for a walk. I don't do enough for my little guy. Could you sign here, please?"[69]

So much for defusing a difficult customer service problem! A dog biscuit is a small thing, but on this day, it made a big difference.

Ask God to show you today what small variations you might make that could improve the overall quality of your life, your family, your business, your church, and your community.

Concentrate on each task, whether trivial or crucial, as if it's the only thing that matters.

I will give them singleness of heart and action.

Jeremiah 32:39

$\mathcal{Y}$ears ago, John McClellan ran for the US Senate in Arkansas. He and his opponent were both scheduled to make a speech at a county fair.

McClellan's opponent spoke first. He blamed McClellan for everything he thought was wrong in the nation, and he got some mild applause at several points. Then at the end of his speech, feeling the heat and humidity of the late-summer day, he picked up the full water pitcher on the railing of the speaker's platform, and began to pour himself a glass of water. He was so busy smiling at the crowd, however, that he momentarily lost sight of what he was doing and poured the water over the railing and down on the head of a white-haired grandmother sitting on the front row in a wheelchair!

McClellan waited while several people helped to dry off the elderly woman. He then said to the crowd: "Do you want a senator who's too dumb to pour water in a glass?"

McClellan won the race.[70]

While striving to meet your goals, don't lose sight of the little things. All those little things added up equal the fulfillment of your goal!

*Show me a man
who cannot bother
to do little things
and I'll show you a
man who cannot be
trusted to do
big things.*

**He who is faithful in a very little
thing is faithful also in much.**

Luke 16:10 NASB

A high school graduate was once hired by a large company to work as a file clerk. After serving in that post for a while, he applied for a position in a department that primarily dealt with statistics. He got the job.

An hour after he began his new assignment, he went to his supervisor. Looking confused and frustrated, he said, "It's these percentages. It's crazy, but I don't remember how to calculate them."

His new supervisor had a sudden revelation that perhaps the personnel department had made a mistake. He didn't want to hurt the young man's feelings, however, so he worked a simple problem for him.

"We had 1200 units of this item in inventory and we shipped 150 of them. To get the percentage of inventory shipped, you divide 150 by 1200. You get .125, or 12.5 percent of the inventory was shipped."

The young man looked at the numbers his boss had scribbled on his note pad and groaned, "Oh, no. Not long division, decimals, and fractions! You don't need me, you need Einstein."[71]

Most people don't get bogged down by the big decisions and problems, but by the little ones. Do the little things well, and the big problems in life rarely show up!

■ ■ ■

Excellence . . . is not an act, but a habit.

Whatever you do, in word or deed, do everything in the name of the Lord Jesus, giving thanks to God the Father through him.

Colossians 3:17 *NRSV*

*W*hen he was six years old, he got up at sunrise to work in the hayfields near his home. By age eight, he was helping his father fix up low-income rental properties, and he was paid a penny for every nail he pulled from old boards. He got his first "real" job at a restaurant in town when he was twelve—clearing tables, washing dishes, and sometimes helping to cook.

He worked from the end of school until ten at night and on Saturdays from two to eleven. It was tough watching his friends run off to play or swim. He didn't particularly like the work he was doing, but he did like the feeling of being able to buy treats for his buddies when they went to the local Tastee Freez.

He gained a reputation for being hard-working and trustworthy. He was granted a line of credit when he was only in the seventh grade! His father, who often worked three jobs, taught him, "If you understand sacrifice and commitment, there are not many things in life you can't have."

He learned that lesson well. With that life philosophy, it's little wonder that J. C. Watts, Jr., (R-Oklahoma) was elected to Congress in 1994.[72]

Many people say that they will do great things for God—someday. Wise people make someday today, and then start by doing what's at hand!

People forget how fast you did a job—but they remember how well you did it.

You are a good and faithful servant. I left you in charge of only a little, but now I will put you in charge of much more.

Matthew 25:21 CEV

*D*uring the Christmas holidays, a woman and her young family were snowbound. Cabin fever was setting in. Then, to make matters worse, the television set went out. In desperation, the woman called a repair shop from the Yellow Pages, and to her surprise, a repairman quickly arrived at her home. He cheerfully climbed over the three restless children and their toys, and went to work.

An hour later, he had reassembled the television and called for her to come and inspect his work. She expected to be handed a bill, but instead, he asked, "What do you think, ma'am?"

"Looks great," she said. "How much do I owe you?"

Instead of writing out the invoice, he just kept staring at the set, admiring his work. "Say, that is a great picture," he said. Then, producing a bottle of cleaning spray from his toolbox, he cleaned the glass on the TV set. He stepped back again, then bent over to the set to remove a missed speck of dust.

From that day on, the woman never called another television repairman. She said, "I liked him simply because he took such pride in his work."[73]

When we truly care about people, we want to do our best for them. If you truly love, you give your best!

■　■　■

Quality is never an accident . . . it represents the wise choice of many alternatives.

Make every effort to add to your faith goodness; and to goodness, knowledge; and to knowledge, self-control; and to self-control, perseverance; and to perseverance, godliness; and to godliness, brotherly kindness; and to brotherly kindness, love.

2 Peter 1:5-7

From the time he heard his first violin recital on the radio at age three, Itzhak Perlman wanted to become a violinist. He began by playing a toy fiddle. Thrilled at his love of music, his parents bought him a secondhand, full-sized violin for six dollars. Despite their limited finances, they arranged for him to take lessons.

Even though Perlman was stricken with poliomyelitis at age four and it took a year for him to recover to the point of using leg braces and crutches, he still practiced his violin every day. At age five, he entered the Tel Aviv Academy of Music. He and his parents later moved to New York City so he could study at Juilliard School for the Performing Arts.

At age eighteen, his debut at Carnegie Hall gained the attention of the world's leading violinists. He won international music competitions and was acclaimed by critics who said, "There is nothing in the whole field of violin playing that he cannot do."

Married and the father of five, Perlman keeps a heavy concert schedule, teaches violin, and raises funds for organizations of people with disabilities. Every aspect of his life is marked by a commitment to quality.[74]

Every person has the option to build a life of quality or mediocrity. Whatever your circumstances, always choose quality!

Information without application leads to frustration.

*Do not merely listen to the word,
and so deceive yourselves.
Do what it says.*

James 1:22

When Les Brown got his first broadcasting job, his primary interest was in becoming a disc jockey. His job, however, was errand boy. But instead of begrudging his low position, he chose to learn and become good at all facets of the broadcasting field!

He served as a music director, a program director, and a production director. He sold airtime. He put together concerts and served as a master of ceremonies. He produced and directed commercials. In short, he became as multitalented and multiskilled as possible.

In contrast, Les knew a man who desired to be a sound technician for recording studios. He had a college degree in sound engineering but when he went in search of a job, he discovered jobs were scarce and difficult to get. The only job offer he got was that of a janitor in a recording studio. He turned down the offer because the money wasn't very good. Years later, he wished he had taken it. At least it would have gotten him in the door so he might show someone what he could do.[75]

In every area of life, we are called to learn and then do. The two are meant to go together. That's especially true in your spiritual walk. It's not enough to know God. We must live out our faith day by day. It's the combination of belief and action that creates a positive impact.

■ ■ ■

Opportunities are usually disguised as hard work, so most people don't recognize them.

Lift up your eyes and look at the fields, for they are already white for harvest!

John 4:35 *NKJV*

om Cruise is one of the most popular actors in America today. What many people don't know, however is that Cruise has dyslexia. Dyslexia is a neurological condition that distorts, or confuses, the way printed words appear on the page.

As a child, Cruise worked hard to compensate for this difference in learning styles, but because of his family's frequent moves, he constantly faced new schools where they were unfamiliar with his reading disability.

At one of the high schools he attended, Cruise won the lead role in *Guys and Dolls*. He felt at home onstage, and he knew then he had found the profession for which he was destined. He would eventually come to be known as one of Hollywood's hardest-working actors.

In each of his roles, Cruise works hard to portray his characters physically as well as psychologically. He spends countless hours learning the speech and body language appropriate for his characters. A producer once said about him, "His road was never paved. It was always full of potholes, and he jumped over all of them."[76]

Nobody lucks into a successful career. When we get excited about what we are doing and work hard at it, our talents will find us opportunities.

I am only one; but still I am one. I cannot do everything, but still I can do something. I will not refuse to do the something I can do.

But Moses said to God, "Who am I that I should go to Pharaoh, and that I should bring the children of Israel out of Egypt?"

Exodus 3:11 NKJV

*L*arry Jones once took a group of pastors to Haiti to do missionary work. As Jones got out of a cab in front of the motel where they were to stay, a young boy asked, "You got a nickel?"

Jones said, "What do you want it for?"

He said, "I haven't eaten all day. If you give me a nickel, I can go to the store and buy a roll."

As Jones dug for change, the boy informed him that for three more pennies, the baker would cut the roll in half and butter it. Jones gave the boy twenty cents, with that he could also get a Coke.

That night, Jones wondered, *What am I going to do with this?* He knew that in his home state of Oklahoma, the storage of tons of surplus wheat was costing American taxpayers millions of dollars. "We ought to take that grain and use it to feed hungry people," he concluded.

Farmers responded to his message by giving him truckloads of wheat. Another farmer volunteered to haul the wheat to Miami where it could be put on a boat and sent to Haiti.

And that's how an organization called Feed the Children was born. Feed the Children now provides food for 100,000 hungry children around the world every day.[77]

One person truly can move a mountain of need, one shovelful at a time.

■ ■ ■

*I'd rather have
1 percent of one
hundred men's
efforts than
100 percent
of my own.*

**So we rebuilt the wall till all of it
reached half its height, for the
people worked with all their heart.**

Nehemiah 4:6

*O*ne day a salesman was driving on a country road when he suddenly found himself stuck in a ditch. He asked a nearby farmer for help. The farmer hitched up Elmo, his blind mule, to the salesman's car. The farmer then grabbed a switch, snapped it in the air, and yelled, "Go, Sam, go!" He snapped it again. "Go, Jackson, go!" Then he flicked his mule and said, "Go, Elmo, go!"

Elmo then proceeded to pull the car out of the ditch.

"Who are 'Sam' and 'Jackson'?" asked the bewildered driver. "Look," the farmer replied, "if Elmo didn't think he had some help, he wouldn't even try!"[78]

Teamwork is important for getting many jobs done efficiently. Yet many Christians never think to ask others to help them or pray for them in their times of need.

A scout troop leader once had this truth plainly illustrated for him. A tree had fallen across a hiking trail and he struggled to move it. "Are you using all your strength?" one of the scouts asked. "Yes," the leader said in exasperation.

"No, I don't think so," the scout replied. "You haven't asked us to help you."[79]

Don't try to go it alone in life. The body of Christ is intended to be just that—a body.

Team spirit is what gives so many companies an edge over their competitors.

They helped every one his neighbour; and every one said to his brother, Be of good courage.

Isaiah 41:6 *KJV*

*K*iller Bees is the name of the boys' high school basketball team in Bridgehampton, New York. Between 1980 and 1993, they amassed a record of 164 wins and only 32 losses, qualified for the state championship playoffs six times, won the championship twice, and finished in the final four two other times. Not at all bad for a school whose entire male student body numbers fewer than twenty!

The coach of the team once said, "I don't really know why we did so well. None of the players was ever really a standout, but they always seemed to play pretty well together. I think the community has a lot to do with it. They really back this team—and have for years. Fathers, brothers, and cousins have played on earlier teams, and mothers, sisters, and aunts relentlessly cheer them on."

The Bees have to be the ultimate in versatility, flexibility, and speed. Their game is "team basketball." They are driven by a commitment to bring honor to their town. Academic performance is high. And they work hard, practicing 365 days a year. As one person noted, "They expect to win and they win."[80]

Wherever you work, whatever you do, you can help cultivate team spirit. In the home, on the job, and in your church—team spirit gives you the winning edge!

■ ■ ■

The important thing to recognize is that it takes a team, and the team ought to get credit for the wins and losses. Successes have many fathers, failures have none.

I planted, Apollos watered, but God gave the growth.
1 Corinthians 3:6 NRSV

*O*ne pleasant afternoon, missionaries in the Philippines set up a croquet game in their front yard. Several of their neighbors became interested and wanted to join in the fun. The missionaries explained the basics of the game to them and started them out, giving each a mallet and ball.

As the game progressed, one of the players had an opportunity to gain an advantage over another player by knocking that person's ball out of the court. The missionary explained the rule, but his advice puzzled the player.

"Why would I want to knock his ball out of the court?" he asked.

"So you will be the winner," the missionary said.

The man shook his head, bewildered. His people lived as hunters and gatherers. They survived not by competing, but by sharing equally in every activity.

The game continued, but no one followed the missionaries' coaching advice. When a player finished moving his ball through all the wickets, the game wasn't over for him. He went back and gave advice to his fellows. This continued until the final player moved through the last wicket, at which point all of the players shouted happily, "We won! We won!"[81]

Do you see your coworkers as teammates or competitors? Become a team player—then everyone wins!

*A team should
be an extension
of the coach's
personality.*

*Christ also suffered for us, leaving us an
example, that ye should follow his steps.*

1 Peter 2:21 *KJV*

*L*egendary football coach George Allen once told the President's Council on Physical Fitness: "No matter who you are or what your position, you must keep fighting for whatever you desire to achieve." Allen lived those words.

As a head coach in the NFL, he took two last-place teams—first the Los Angeles Rams and then the Washington Redskins—from the cellar to the Super Bowl.

Retired and now seventy-two, Allen received a call from Long Beach State University, pleading with him to rescue their ailing football program. They told Allen they would have to cancel their entire football program if he didn't help them. "All right," he said. "I'll do it."

When Allen arrived, the football squad was low on morale, facilities, and funds. They were the laughingstock of the campus. He set out to rebuild the team, setting the pace by running laps and doing sit-ups and push-ups right alongside his players. He demanded performance; he lectured hard. He instilled intensity, focus, and desire.

For the first time in years, LBSU had a winning season. Six weeks after the final game of the season, a 29-20 win over UNLV, Allen died of a heart attack. He had fought to the very end, and won.[82]

Jesus, Who is our coach and example, lived and died victoriously so that we can do the same.

■　　■　　■

Management's job is to see the company not as it is . . . but as it can become.

You are Peter, and on this rock I will build my church, and the gates of Hades will not prevail against it.

Matthew 16:18 NRSV

When Arturo was eight, his parents separated, his mother went on welfare, and he struggled to learn English. Even so, he made the honor roll. He was one of some 500 children in one of the poorest school districts in Texas to display this kind of success.

The person behind these successful children is principal Velda Correa, who made a habit of knocking on doors in her district to ask, "What can your school do for you?" She then focused her efforts on meeting the needs she uncovered.

She kept the school open on Saturdays to help students catch up on missed days. She enlisted the help of the school librarian to help the students practice English by reading to them and drilling them with questions. The school counselors took on more work. Every teacher became involved in helping to direct a theatrical or musical production. The result? Attendance is well above 90 percent and the students are scoring higher on state exams.

Correa has said, "It doesn't matter if you have the richest campus or the poorest. It's what you do with what you've got." Correa saw the potential in her students and did her best to develop it.[83]

Jesus sees the potential in each person and seeks to magnify it. Are you willing to see and develop the potential in yourself?

An effective organization has a purpose that is shared by all its members and to which they will willingly commit their efforts. People working together can do almost anything.

We continually remember before our God and Father your work produced by faith, your labor prompted by love, and your endurance inspired by hope in our Lord Jesus Christ.

1 Thessalonians 1:3

*A*mong the "casualties" of the 1992 Los Angeles riots, which occurred in the aftermath of the Rodney King verdict, was a FEDCO store. Its interior and the structure itself were totally destroyed. Experts said it would take nine months to a year to make it operational again.

FEDCO executives called a summit meeting with the union employees, 80 percent of whom were minorities. They met with suppliers. Their message? "There are 1,300 jobs at stake here. They say we can't do it. We don't have the skills. We don't have the energy. We don't have the will. We don't have the guts. We don't care. We aren't good enough. Well, are they right?"

The answer came back a resounding, "No!"

The community did what the experts said would take nine months in only eighteen days! When the store was ready to reopen, nearly 2,000 customers were in line waiting to be part of the miracle. The grand reopening ceremonies included a forty-five-voice employee choir, who encouraged the audience to join in. The choir number swelled to 450, and there wasn't a dry eye in the house.[84]

Can you imagine what we might do to further the Kingdom of God if we banded together with that kind of focus? Focus is always a key to winning.

The leader seeks to communicate his vision to his followers.

Moses went up from the plains of Moab to Mount Nebo, to the top of Pisgah . . . and the LORD showed him the whole land.

Deuteronomy 34:1 NRSV

A young man who was put back a year in school was labeled "mentally handicapped." Fortunately for him, one of the people he encountered in the wake of this setback was a man named LeRoy Washington. He was the school's speech and drama teacher. Known for his powerful presence and kind reputation, Mr. Washington noticed the young man who attended his classes and rehearsals without being officially enrolled.

One day, he called upon the young man to write something on the blackboard for him. "I can't do that, sir," he said.

"Why not?" the teacher asked. The youth was embarrassed to admit why, but it finally came out that he was in the special education class. "It doesn't matter," Washington said. "Go to the board and follow my directions." The youth said, "I can't. I'm educable mentally retarded."

Washington seized the moment. He rose from his desk, gazed long and hard at the young man, and then said, "Do not ever say that again. Someone's opinion of you does not have to become your reality."

"In that moment," Les Brown says, "my life began to follow a new course."[85]

A winner not only has a vision for his own life, but can also inspire those with whom he lives, works, and worships. Ask God to enlarge your vision today.

■ ■ ■

It's not what you tell your players that counts. It's what they hear.

For the ear tests words as the palate tastes food.

Job 34:3 NRSV

A Dodgers farm club team coached by Tommy Lasorda was leading Tucson by one run in the eighth inning, and Tucson had the bases loaded with two outs. Lasorda felt the time was right for a pep talk with his pitcher, Bobby O'Brien.

Lasorda slowly walked out to the mound and said, "Bobby, if the heavens opened up right now and you could hear the voice of the Big Dodger in the sky and he said to you, 'Bobby, you're going to die and come up to heaven, and this is the last batter you're ever going to face,' how would you like to meet the Lord, getting this man out or letting him get a hit from you?"

O'Brien said, "I'd want to face Him getting this guy out."

"That's right, you would. Now, how do you know that after you throw the next pitch you're not going to die? This might be the last hitter you're ever going to face." And Lasorda walked away.

Before he even got to the dugout, however, a batter smacked a base hit to right field, driving in two runs. "Bobby, what happened?" Lasorda asked him later. O'Brien said, "You had me so worried about dying I couldn't concentrate on the batter!"[86]

What message are you communicating to your friends, family, and coworkers? Be careful to think before you speak, and listen to what you're saying to be sure it is what you intend for them to hear.

If I went back to college again, I'd concentrate on . . . learning to write and to speak before an audience. Nothing in life is more important than the ability to communicate effectively.

Death and life are in the power of the tongue.
Proverbs 18:21 NRSV

*M*any analysts of today's business climate consider communication the most vital tool of any salesman, manager, or executive. A man who has a key position in a large accounting firm in Chicago is a good example of this opinion. He has never studied accounting. He has a master's degree in English literature. Many people, however, regard him as the only person in his corporation who speaks English. His job is to take the numbers and facts compiled by the accountants and communicate them to the customers. He writes the final reports in language a nonaccountant can understand. He makes a very good living as the firm's designated communicator.

People in the sports world have also come to recognize the importance of communication. It can make a tremendous difference in earning power.

Boxer Sugar Ray Leonard is a superb communicator, for example. Even when he lost in the ring, his outgoing, articulate personality won him promotional contracts worth millions![87]

How do you rate yourself as a communicator? Can you motivate others with your words? Are you a good listener? Do you ask the right questions? Take a course in communication. Ask God to show you how you might improve your communication skills. They are another key on the key chain of a winner.

■   ■   ■

*Our success
didn't come out
of a computer.
It came out of
the sweat glands
of our coaches
and players.*

**Forgetting what lies behind and straining
forward to what lies ahead, I press on
toward the goal for the prize of the
heavenly call of God in Christ Jesus.**

Philippians 3:13-14 *NRSV*

*B*orn in crime-riddled East St. Louis, Jaqueline grew up with several strikes against her. Still, she had dreams. When she was nine years old, she entered her first track-and-field competition. She finished last. She took her defeat as a challenge, however, and in her next meet, she performed better. She continued to work hard and one day she came home exclaiming, "I got first place!"

In high school, she went out for track, volleyball, and basketball. She studied hard, and graduated in the top 10 percent of her class. Then, when she was a freshman in college, her mother died. Her world was shattered.

A young UCLA coach helped Jackie overcome her grief through hard work—training for the heptathlon. Then, two more blows struck. In 1983, Jackie pulled a hamstring and she learned that she was very allergic, which caused her to have exercise-induced asthma. She didn't stop working though, she just worked differently.

By 1984, she was competing again. In 1988 and in 1992 Jaqueline Joyner-Kersee won Olympic gold in the heptathlon, and in 1996, a bronze in the long jump. Hard work earned her the title of the greatest female athlete in the world.[88]

Most people have a multitude of excuses for their laziness and lack of achievement. Winners are not lazy and they don't make excuses. Retire your old standbys today!

■ ■ ■

I was taught that everything is attainable if you're prepared to give up, to sacrifice, to get it.

For if we are faithful to the end, trusting God just as we did when we first became Christians, we will share in all that belongs to Christ.

Hebrews 3:14 *TLB*

*G*ary Player won more international golf tournaments in his hey-day than any other player of his time. Today, he continues to win on the senior tour. A man once said to him, "I'd give anything if I could hit a golf ball like you."

Tired and frustrated after a day of poor play, Player replied, "No, you wouldn't. Do you know what you've got to do to hit a golf ball like me? You've got to get up at five o'clock in the morning, go out on the course, and hit one thousand golf balls. Your hand starts bleeding, and you walk up to the clubhouse, wash the blood off your hand, slap a bandage on it, and go out and hit another one thousand golf balls. That's what it takes."

Echoing this sentiment, a football coach once told his players at a summer camp, "Now, guys, you're going to get out there in the hot sun and you're going to be working and the coach is going to be fussing at you and you're going to feel like you're going to die. But when you feel like you're going to die, just keep working. Because the good Lord put a little mechanism in your head that makes you pass out before you die. If you do pass out, we'll drag you up to the dressing room and put you in the shower and give you some salt tablets so you'll be ready for the next practice."[89]

Most people wish. Winners act. Quit taking your chances at the wishing well and start taking action. That's how a winner becomes the master of his destiny.

■　■　■

People who have attained things worth having in this world have worked while others have idled, have persevered when others gave up in despair.

Lazy people want much but get little, while the diligent are prospering.

Proverbs 13:4 TLB

*I*n a fertile valley, two brothers named Asa and Ira lived side by side on their farms. One day Asa said to his brother, "Do you see what a hold the weeds are taking?"

Ira said, "We must be resigned. Weeds as well as grain are part of the Creator's plan." Then he went to take his afternoon nap.

"I can only be resigned to what I cannot help," Asa said. So he went to work, ploughing and hoeing until his fields were clear of the weeds.

Yet another day Asa said to Ira, "The armyworm is in the neighborhood. It's coming our way." Ira said, "I'm going to pray the worms change course." Asa said, "I will pray, also, for strength to do the work that must be done." And he dug a protective trench around his land.

Still another morning Asa noted, "The river is rising. Our farms are in danger of being flooded." Ira said, "It's a judgment from God. There's nothing we can do but hope." Asa quickly went to build a dike.

In the end, he had a tremendous harvest, and Ira had very little. "Why are you so prosperous?" Ira asked his brother.

"I never presumed to send a petition upward," Asa replied, "without making toil the messenger of my prayer."[90]

Work and prayer go together. One is never an adequate substitute for the other.

■   ■   ■

If your desk isn't cluttered, you probably aren't doing your job.

Be diligent . . . a worker who does not need to be ashamed.

2 Timothy 2:15 NKJV

*O*ne of the most successful catalog businesses in America is the Lillian Vernon Corporation, which ships more than $238 million in goods every year. Few people know, however, that Lillian Vernon is a real person or that her business began as a tiny mail-order business she operated from her home in Mount Vernon, New York. It was launched with gift money she received as a wedding present in 1949.

While many women see little crossover in their work lives and home lives, Vernon actually credits her success to performing both roles simultaneously. She believes many women make great managers in business because they have gained valuable experience in dealing with multiple distractions.

Time management is an essential skill in business, and it is something that most working mothers and wives become very adept at. Vernon believes she honed her own valuable skills by running her household and business at the same time.

She has said, "Once you've dressed a struggling infant in a snowsuit, argued about the gas bill, and composed an enticing ad—all while the meatloaf baked in the oven—the rest is a breeze."[91]

Whether your desk is cluttered or not, you probably have a certain amount of clutter in your life. Ask God to show you how to work all the pieces together. He is a God of order.

Few people think more than two or three times a year. I have made an international reputation by thinking once or twice a week.

Mary treasured all these words and pondered them in her heart.

Luke 2:19 NRSV

*I*f you study the lives of the truly great individuals who have influenced the world, you will find that in virtually every case, they spent considerable amounts of time alone—contemplating, meditating, listening. Every outstanding religious leader in history spent time in solitude. As we see in the gospels, Jesus frequently went off by Himself to pray.

The same is true in the political world. Churchill, Disraeli, Roosevelt, Lincoln, and many others have openly stated the benefits they gained from spending time alone. Most leading universities require professors to lecture only a few hours per week, leaving them time to think and conduct research.[92]

When a person is alone, he or she can sort through the past and put it into perspective. There's time to envision the future and make plans for getting there.

Above all, time alone can be beneficial in building one's relationship with God. Take time to pray and reflect on the Scriptures. Create a space of your own where you can go periodically to sit in silence. You may find this space by taking a walk or by turning part of an attic or shed into your own private study.

Set aside at least half an hour for silence. Determine not to worry or plan or work during that time—just listen. God is always ready and willing to speak to you, He's just waiting for you to incline your ear.

More important than victory is effort. At the center of effort is courage.

Although Daniel knew that the document had been signed, he continued to go to his house, which had windows in its upper room open toward Jerusalem, and to get down on his knees three times a day to pray to his God and praise him, just as he had done previously.

Daniel 6:10 NRSV

*J*oan Curtis was at a crossroads. As a diversion, she went to see a special exhibit by Lamar Dodd, a well-known Atlanta artist. She had worked at a university for years, but she longed to open her own business.

She and her husband met Dodd at the exhibition and he invited them to his home. Over coffee, he unexpectedly said to her, "You're frightened. I know the symptoms."

"That's hard for me to imagine," she said. "Why?" he replied, "I've been frightened all my life. But courage is no more than cussed stubbornness, and I've plenty of that. It means getting up each day and doing what you have to, going on when circumstances get you down, pushing ahead when others hold you back." Dodd shared how he broke his fear by promising himself he'd work at his craft every day, no matter how he felt.

Curtis and Dodd became friends and she saw him a number of times, one time shortly after he had a stroke that paralyzed his right hand, his painting hand. Even so, he went to a canvas that day, placed a brush between two fingers, and with his left hand guiding the brush, pushed it across the canvas, leaving a perfect line of color. Courage? Yes. And just plain stubbornness.[93]

Take courage or, stubbornly refuse to give up on your dream. Do something today that moves you closer to your goal.

■   ■   ■

The important thing in the Olympic games is not winning but taking part.

Here am I; send me!
Isaiah 6:8 *NRSV*

*O*n a PBS television special, author Leo Buscaglia once talked about the great appreciation he has for Julia Child, the legendary culinary personality. He said, "I just love her attitude. She says, 'Tonight we're going to make a soufflé!' And she beats this and whisks that, and she drops things on the floor. She wipes her face with her napkin and does all these wonderful human things. Then she takes the soufflé and throws it in the oven and talks to you for awhile. Finally, she says, 'Now it's ready!' But when she opens the oven, the soufflé just falls flat as a pancake! But does she panic or burst into tears? No! She smiles and says, 'Well, you can't win 'em all. Bon appetit!'"[94]

At times, you may feel as if your dream is some kind of soufflé in the making. You whip up new ideas and beat out new plans, then put your dream to the heat of hard work, all in hopes of success, and sometimes even your best efforts fall flat. What do you do?

Beating yourself up over a failure will get you nowhere. A much more beneficial approach is learning what you can from the experience and pressing forward to try again.

Winning is not defined by what you accomplish, but by how you play the game you choose to play.

You have the greatest chance of winning when your first commitment is to a total and enthusiastic involvement in the game itself. Enthusiasm is what matters most.

It is good to be zealous in a good thing.
Galatians 4:18 *NKJV*

At age five, Chris had a two-line part in a school play. Thrilled at the applause he received, he announced upon returning home that he wanted to be an actor when he grew up. His mother explained to him that acting was a difficult job. And she knew that few parts existed for someone like Chris, who has Down's syndrome.

At his birth, Chris' mother had been told her son would never learn to walk or talk, much less lead a satisfying life. She was advised to put him in an institution. She refused to give up on her son, however. She walked with him, talked to him, and read to him. As a preschooler Chris could both walk and talk and was keenly interested in other people and sensitive to their needs. He could sing TV commercials and liked to imitate *Sesame Street* characters.

As a young teen, Chris looked at a UPS truck and said, "I have Up syndrome, because I feel happy and excited about my life."

It was that attitude that eventually led to Chris Burke being cast in the part of Corky in the very successful TV series, *Life Goes On*.[95]

Do you have "up" syndrome, or "down" syndrome? God's Word teaches us to rejoice at all times, and give thanks. When we live God's way, we are living with "up" syndrome, and we can spread it to others.

■　　■　　■

Never complain about what you permit.

A man's own folly ruins his life,
yet his heart rages against the LORD.

Proverbs 19:3

*T*he story is told about a dog that was sitting on its master's porch one day. The dog was moaning and groaning, and occasionally, he broke out into a loud whine. All the while the dog's owner quietly rocked nearby, seemingly unconcerned. A man walking by the house asked why the dog was acting that way.

The dog's owner said, "Because he's lying on a nail." The man asked, "Well, why doesn't he get off it?" The owner said, "Because it's not hurting bad enough."

We've all encountered people who are like that dog. They moan and groan about their jobs, their circumstances, their situations, but they never seem to have enough energy to do something about any of it. They aren't yet sick and tired of being sick and tired.

Each of us is born with the power to change our attitude, and very often, change the circumstances that we don't like. We do not have to be victims of the words "but," "woulda," "coulda," and "shoulda."

Authors John Roger and Peter McWilliams were wise when they wrote: "'But' is a crutch; it is an excuse for procrastinators. . . . It allows us to validate our inaction. When hard times hit . . . look for reasons to move forward, not for reasons to idle through life."[96]

Men grow making decisions and assuming responsibility for them.

So then every one of us shall give account of himself to God.

Romans 14:12 *KJV*

*T*here are three parts to decision-making: make it, make it yours, and die by it. A woman named Mary lived this out. Sixteen, pregnant, and unmarried, she fled to an uncle's home where she worked for her room and board until her baby arrived. A childless middle-aged couple offered to adopt her son.

"No. I am woman enough to have that baby," she replied, "and I will be woman enough to raise him." She did accept the couple's offer to keep her child while she worked to save money so the two of them could return home.

The couple agreed, sure they'd seen the last of the young mother. They were wrong, however. After a year of working as a domestic maid for five dollars a week, Mary took custody of her baby and made the trip home.

Mary was married a short time later, and over the years she had five more children. She gave them a home filled with love and gratitude to a good God. Each of her children graduated from college. Faye became a music teacher; Barbara, a mortgage banker; Lois, a nurse; Nancy, a music therapist; and Elizabeth, a physical therapist.

And the firstborn son? Cleve Francis became a medical doctor and country singer.[97]

You may not always make good decisions, but you can "make" every decision into good by the way you live it out.

I often tell my son: "If 'ifs' and 'buts' were candy and nuts, we'd all have a Merry Christmas!"

But they all alike began to make excuses.
Luke 14:18

A retiring corporate chairman was turning over the reins of the company to his successor. After the board meeting, the old chairman took the new chairman aside and said, "I have two pieces of advice to give you," and he slipped him two envelopes. One was marked "Number 1" and the other "Number 2."

"Keep these sealed envelopes," he said. "And do not share them with anyone. If a crisis develops that you can't solve, open Number 1 and it will tell you what to do. Keep the second envelope and use it only if you have another major crisis."

A couple of years passed and a crisis occurred that endangered the new chairman's career. Not knowing what to do, he remembered the two envelopes. He went to his safe and took out the first one and opened it. It said, "Blame your predecessor." He followed the advice and got out of the jam.

A couple more years passed and another crisis arose. He remembered the second envelope and went to his safe to retrieve it. This one said, "Prepare two envelopes!"[98]

You can either become an excuse maker or a decisive, faith-filled winner. Make today the day you set aside your excuses and start doing the things you know to do.

■ ■ ■

*Change your
thoughts and
you change
your world.*

**The mind of sinful man is death,
but the mind controlled by the
Spirit is life and peace.**

Romans 8:6

$\mathcal{A}$ man once went diving with his brother off the coast of Bora Bora. Two other divers accompanied them on the boat—a man and his ten-year-old son. The father kept asking, "Are there any sharks around here?" Everyone kept reassuring him, "No, nothing dangerous, nothing to worry about."

As the father and son plunged into the water, one of the other men said, "I hope that guy is going to be okay." He knew that they would almost certainly see sharks.

Although they were diving in a lagoon and not on the outer reef, the lagoon was known to be full of white-tip reef sharks. They felt justified in their reassurances to the man, however, because these sharks are not considered dangerous unless directly provoked.

As the father took pictures underwater in the coral, a white-tip swam by. Soon other sharks appeared. They passed to his left and right, gliding over him and under him. He probably had a dozen encounters within ten minutes.

Back on the boat, all he said was, "Beautiful dive, wasn't it?" The others agreed, "Beautiful." He then said, "Thank God I didn't see any sharks. I don't know what I would have done if I had."[99]

Most often, we receive what we expect to receive. Expect good things from God. He's waiting to give them to you.

■ ■ ■

The last of the human freedoms is to choose one's attitude in any given set of circumstances.

Consider it all joy, my brethren, when you encounter various trials, knowing that the testing of your faith produces endurance.

James 1:2-3 *NASB*

*A*ccording to an old fable, the devil had decided to pack it up and go out of business. He planned to put all of his tools out for a sidewalk sale and sell them to whomever would pay the price.

On the night of the big sale, all of the tools were attractively displayed. Among them were malice, hate, envy, jealousy, greed, sensuality, and deceit. Off to the side lay a harmless-looking wedge-shaped tool which had obviously been used a great deal.

A potential buyer asked the devil, "What's that? It's priced so much higher than all of the other tools which aren't nearly as worn."

"That's discouragement," the devil answered.

"But why is it priced so high?" the customer asked.

"Because that's the tool I used to pry open a person's consciousness when I couldn't get near him with any of the other tools. Once discouragement got me inside, I could let all the other tools do their work."[100]

No matter what successes we have in life, almost everyone experiences discouragement, sometimes on a daily basis. You can control your attitude. Choose to remain positive and faith-filled by tanking up on God's Word. If the devil can't discourage you, he can't defeat you.

■   ■   ■

The greatest revolution of our generation is the discovery that human beings, by changing the inner attitudes of their minds, can change the outer aspects of their lives.

As he thinks in his heart, so is he.
Proverbs 23:7 *NKJV*

*W*hen Kent Culler arrived in the world a couple of months prematurely, he wasn't breathing. The doctors gave him a heavy dose of oxygen to save his life, but the life-preserving oxygen caused Kent to be blind.

Although their son was sight-impaired, Kent's parents were determined that he not be life-impaired. They taught him to do virtually everything other children did: climb trees, ride a bicycle, and go to school. He had mishaps (what child doesn't?), but he was also a straight-A student and he became a Boy Scout. His favorite book was *The Golden Book of Astronomy.*

Kent graduated valedictorian of his high school class, was Phi Beta Kappa in college, and earned a doctorate in physics. In his early twenties, he submitted a computer model to NASA that improved the space shuttle's radar system.

Today, Kent Culler is one of NASA's most creative and productive scientists. Unlike many blind people who grow up being told what they cannot do, Kent Culler grew up believing he could do anything he wanted to do. As a result, the whole universe belongs to him![101]

What do you believe you can do? That's the outer limit of what you will do. Maybe it's time to increase your belief.

There is no more miserable human being than the one in whom nothing is habitual but indecision.

Elijah went before the people and said, "How long will you waver between two opinions?"

1 Kings 18:21

*T*he story is told of a Maine potato farmer who hired extra help during harvesttime. He had a pile of potatoes in his farmyard that was six feet high and long enough to fill a wagon. He told his new farmhand to divide the potatoes into two piles—big ones in one pile and little ones in another.

At noon, the farmer came back to check on the man's progress and was surprised to find that he hadn't moved a single potato in almost four hours. He was shocked by this incredible display of laziness. He demanded to know why the man hadn't done anything.

The hired man grimaced as if in great pain and said, "It's not that moving potatoes is hard. It's all these decisions that are holding me back."

The homespun philosopher Elbert Hubbard once said, "No executive can afford to have it said about him, 'The only time he ever takes a stand is on the bathroom scale.'"[102]

Some people are afraid to make decisions because they think every decision is irreversible. In reality, virtually any decision can be remade if it proves to be a bad one. Very few decisions are life-and-death in importance.

Inability to decide shows a lack of faith. Trust God to help you make the right decisions and don't delay. Decide.

In any moment of decision the best thing you can do is the right thing. The worst thing you can do is nothing.

I have resolved what to do.
Luke 16:4 NKJV

Olympic gold-medal figure skater Ekaterina Gordeeva seemed to have a storybook life. She married her skating partner and "prince," Sergei Grinkov and then gave birth to a beautiful baby daughter, Daria. When Grinkov died suddenly at the age of twenty-eight during a skating practice in Lake Placid, New York, she felt as if the sun had set in her life.

Ekaterina returned to Moscow for her husband's funeral and slid into a deep depression. She didn't seem to have any purpose in her life. Then her mother jolted her back to her senses when she said, "Daria doesn't need a sick mother. Whether you live in Moscow or go back to America, try to be a healthy person again."

Ekaterina began to skate again, relearning how to skate solo rather than as a pair. She felt close to Sergei when she was on the ice, and she found that comforting.

In 1996, the skating community asked Ekaterina to skate in a tribute they were giving to Sergei. She chose as her music Mahler's Symphony No. 5, which the composer had written as a love letter to his future wife. She skated from her heart, and she received a standing ovation. Ekaterina had returned to the ice, making a definitive decision to go forward in life.[103]

What decision do you need to make that will lead you to greater depths of faith and greater heights of winning?

■ ■ ■

A leader is a person who knows what to do next; knows why it's important to do it; and knows how to get the job done!

And David shepherded them with integrity of heart; with skillful hands he led them.

Psalm 78:72

*D*r. Bill Foege, a devout Christian doctor, is one of the world's foremost experts in disease prevention. He was instrumental in the eradication of smallpox in 1977, was the head of the Centers for Disease Control for almost ten years, and later served as executive director of The Carter Center. He often turned down high-paying jobs so that he might serve people in remote areas of the world.

Once while in the deep jungle of Biafra, he faced the challenge of immunizing hundreds of people scattered in small, isolated villages. He went to the regional chief, explained the program, and asked for a guide to take him to the various villages. The chief looked up at him and said, "No, it will be easier if we bring them all here," and he directed his drummer to send a message.

The next morning, streams of people crowded into the village square. "How in the world did you induce them to come here just for an immunization program?" Dr. Foege asked. The chief replied, "I told them to come if they wanted to see the tallest man in the world." Dr. Foege is six-foot, seven-inches tall.[104]

You may use various methods for getting a job done, but don't be varied in your mission.

■   ■   ■

A prime function of a leader is to keep hope alive.

They strengthened the souls of the disciples and encouraged them to continue in the faith.

Acts 14:22 NRSV

*T*hings weren't looking good for the ballet in Waterville, Maine, in 1995. The troupe, led by former Russian ballet star Andrei Bossov, received standing ovations for its productions, but bankruptcy loomed in the wings and checks began to bounce. Bossov returned to Russia.

But then, the Marines arrived in the person of Colonel Michael Wyly. Retired from military service, he had grown to love ballet between trips to the battlefield in Vietnam. And, his thirteen-year-old daughter had studied with Bossov. So Wyly intervened for the ailing ballet company, persuading Bossov to return and form a new company—the Bossov Ballet Theatre.

Then, Wyly called in reinforcements—his old Marine buddies. Most of them didn't know anything about ballet, but whatever he asked of them, they did. One former private who lives in Houston said, "If Mike Wyly asks you to do something, you just pack your gear and go."

Wyly formed an all-Marine board of directors, which "meets" on the Internet. They scout ballet schools, raise money, and maintain a corporate structure. Wyly taught Bossov the Marine motto: *semper fidelis*—"always faithful." "Marines will always be here for you," he said.[105]

When you give people hope, they can accomplish anything. Be a hope-giver to those around you today!

■   ■   ■

Your tongue can destroy or build, tear up or mend. Use your words to build confidence in others.

The one who guards his mouth preserves his life; the one who opens wide his lips comes to ruin.

Proverbs 13:3 NASB

A woman who was scheduled to speak as part of a college leadership program was assured that housing would be provided for her campus visit. When she arrived, however, she discovered that she had been assigned to a dorm room for her two-night stay. She was dismayed to find that the room didn't have a phone and the shower, besides being down the hall, was cold. She longed for both room service and maid service. Not wanting to appear to be a snob, she quietly slipped out of the dorm and checked into a local hotel at her own expense.

The morning of her departure from the college, she was waiting in the lobby of the hotel for a shuttle to the airport. Another would-be shuttle passenger came into the lobby, and she began to make small talk with him. As she chattered away about her experience at the college, she included details of the uncomfortable dorm room and her move to the hotel. Finally she stopped talking long enough to ask the man, "And what do you do?"

He said, "I am the president of the college."[106]

It always pays to listen at least twice as much as you speak. Then, when you speak, you won't say anything you will regret. Practice really listening to people. It's harder than you think, but the benefits are well worth the effort.

The leader . . . demonstrates confidence that the challenge can be met, the need resolved, the crisis overcome.

Be strong and courageous; do not be frightened or dismayed, for the LORD your God is with you wherever you go.

Joshua 1:9 NRSV

$\mathcal{A}$s a college freshman, John Hockenberry was in an automobile accident that left him confined to a wheelchair. He said of his realization that he would never walk again, "My body now was capable of less, but virtually all of what it could do was suddenly charged with meaning."

John decided to transfer from Chicago to the University of Oregon where winters were mild and he wouldn't have to battle snow-packed sidewalks.

In 1980, he became a student volunteer for KLCC, a campus radio station affiliated with National Public Radio. He worked on reports for NPR when Mount St. Helens erupted and was soon sent on other regional assignments. No one even knew he used a wheelchair until the day he missed a deadline for lack of a wheelchair-accessible pay phone.

In 1981, John went to work for NPR full-time as a newscaster on the popular program, *All Things Considered*. In the 1990s, he worked for ABC and CNBC. Then, in 1996 he joined NBC news.

He has said of his disability that it taught him "life can be reinvented." While some saw him standing on a ledge and not jumping off, John always said he saw himself as "climbing up to get a better view."[107]

Any crisis you face can be overcome. "How?" is your challenge of discovery. Ask God for His wisdom in every crisis, act on it, and you will be an overcomer.

■　　■　　■

It may be all right to be content with what you have; never with what you are.

Anyone who thinks he is standing strong should be careful not to fall.

1 Corinthians 10:12 *NCV*

*I*n 1963, Patty Duke became the youngest performer ever to win an Academy Award for Best Supporting Actress. Yet despite her professional success, she was deeply unhappy. From childhood, she experienced panic attacks. At age eighteen, she had a severe manic episode followed by a terrible depression.

In the years that followed, Duke managed to function as an actress, but her personal life was in shambles. She sought help from a psychiatrist who diagnosed her with manic-depressive disorder and prescribed medication. Within three weeks, she began to improve, feeling a calmness she had never known.

While the medication didn't solve all her problems, she learned to deal with those that remained. She since has won three Emmy Awards for her roles in made-for-television movies, and by talking about her mental illness, she has offered hope for thousands of people.[108]

Today, many people suffer in silence with problems that they alone know about. We should be willing to open ourselves up and talk about our inner struggles—both to God and to other compassionate people—so that we might be healed and thereby encourage others. That's a key to growth in every area of life.

It is the capacity to develop and improve their skills that distinguishes leaders from their followers.

And Jesus increased in wisdom and stature, and in favour with God and man.

Luke 2:52 *KJV*

*A*s well as being an expert in the business of manufacturing envelopes, motivational author and speaker Harvey Mackay is a student of languages. He has studied about half a dozen of them, one of which is Chinese.

On a business trip to China, he had a great opportunity to use it. As the leader of a business delegation, he made international news by being the first post-World War II American businessman to deliver a speech in Chinese in that nation.

As the result of that trip, he made a number of contacts with American businessmen—primarily because they appreciated his resourcefulness. They may not have known anything about Chinese, or the envelope business, but they decided that if someone had taken the trouble to learn a difficult language, that person was most likely willing to learn more about their business needs and come up with innovative solutions.

By speaking Chinese he sold, in his words, "a whale of a lot of envelopes."[109]

Keep growing, learning, and changing. Your willingness to listen and to continue learning new things will add to your reputation as a leader and a winner.

It is more than willingness to change that sets the true leaders apart. It is seeking out change and wringing every bit of potential out of it that takes you to the next horizon.

If ye have faith as a grain of mustard seed . . . nothing shall be impossible unto you.

Matthew 17:20 KJV

illiam was only nine years old the first time he caddied. It was the start of a lifelong love affair with golf. By age twelve, he was on the practice fairway.

After he returned home from World War II, all William wanted to do was play golf, but few clubs in the Canton area accepted blacks. He wouldn't be stopped, however. He saw a seventy-eight acre farm covered with weeds and soybeans and envisioned it as a golf course. Two black physicians financed his dream.

William and his wife moved to the farm in 1946. When he wasn't working at his job as a security guard, he worked on clearing the land. It would still be sixteen years before the Professional Golfers Association accepted black members, but William never thought of himself as a pioneer. He simply wanted to play golf.

The Clearview Golf Club in East Canton opened in 1948 as a nine-hole course. William continued working as a security guard for eighteen more years—until he could purchase an additional fifty-two acres and expand the course to eighteen holes.

Today, William Powell is the only black person in America to have designed, built, and owned his own golf course. It is a truly integrated club. That's all he ever really wanted—for everybody to have a chance to play golf.[110]

Don't ever give up. Your dream is not impossible!

■   ■   ■

More men fail through lack of purpose than lack of talent.

Could you not keep awake one hour?
Mark 14:37 NRSV

*W*es Smith wrote a humorous book titled *Welcome to the Real World*—a book of advice for students newly graduated from high school or college and looking for their first "real" jobs. One piece of advice he gives in the book is: "Having a drink with the boys after work every night is a bad idea. Notice that the boss doesn't do it. That is why he is the boss and they are still the boys."

He wrote that with one particular group of party-hardy young business acquaintances in mind. Five years after the book was published, he ran into one of those young men. The man volunteered to Smith that he had read his book and as a result, had decided never to go drinking after work again. It paid off. He had been promoted to a vice presidency at a major savings and loan.[111]

In your drive to reach your dream, you will have many opportunities to party. Jesus was right when He said that a person cannot serve two masters. Those who are serious about success, but are also serious about having "a good time" are divided in their heart. They are not truly focused on their goals.

That is not to say that winners can't have fun. They can, should, and do! But they don't spend their life moving from party to party, they keep their eyes on their goals and move step-by-step to accomplish them.

Remain focused. It's critical to fulfilling your potential.

■   ■   ■

Meetings are indispensable when you don't want to do anything.

While the bridegroom tarried, they all slumbered and slept.

Matthew 25:5 *KJV*

"*D*o you have problem-solving meetings in your company?"

"Of course. We meet every week."

"Are notes taken during the meeting?"

"Yes, we have a secretary who takes notes and then circulates them afterward."

"Then please go back to your offices and return with last week's problem-solving meeting notes. And while you're at it, bring back the notes from six months ago, this week one year ago, and this week two years ago."[112]

Most people who admit to attending regular problem-solving meetings couldn't, or wouldn't want to, follow through on that request. In most organizations, executives and managers have been working on the same list of unresolved problems for months, perhaps years. Often, people purposefully keep their desks piled high with problems to give themselves a false sense of being needed.

Problems are for solving. Don't just baby-sit your problems. Address them, deal with them, and resolve them. The same goes for doubts, questions, and fears. Face them. Search for answers. Take action. That's the true winner's way.

■   ■   ■

There is nothing so useless as doing efficiently that which should not be done at all.

Wherefore do ye spend money for that which is not bread?

Isaiah 55:2 *KJV*

*T*here is a story about a sentry who faithfully stood his post day after day. The guard was dutiful in discharging his responsibility, but there was no obvious reason for his being there.

One day, a passerby asked him why he was standing in that place. "I don't know," the sentry replied, "I'm just following orders." The passerby went on to the sentry's superior and asked him why the sentry was standing there.

"We're just following orders," the captain responded.

The captain then took that question to the king, "Your Highness, why do we post a sentry at that particular spot?" But even the king didn't know the answer. He summoned the wise men and asked them the same question.

Apparently, one hundred years before, Catherine the Great had planted a rosebush on that spot and ordered a sentry to protect it. The rosebush had been dead for eighty years, but the sentry still stood guard.

Author Annie Dillard observed that we are all prone to "diddle around making itsy-bitsy friends and meals and journeys for itsy-bitsy years on end. But," she said, "the world is wider than that in all directions. . . . We are raising tomatoes when we should be raising Cain, or Lazarus."[113]

Nothing is so powerful as an insight into human nature.

Give to Your servant an understanding heart to judge Your people, that I may discern between good and evil.

1 Kings 3:9 *NKJV*

*J*ohn Callahan has a knack for capturing the essence of human stupidity and selfishness—and he makes people laugh in the process. He is a well-known cartoonist. He has also been a quadriplegic since he was injured in a car accident at the age of twenty-one.

For several years after the accident, Callahan felt unhappy and purposeless. When he was twenty-seven years old, he finally had a new insight into his life: His problems were due to a dependence on alcohol, not his quadriplegia.

John had started drinking in high school, and alcohol had become an increasing problem in his life. Even after his injury, he continued to drink with the help of friends who reasoned that it was one of the few "pleasures" he could still enjoy. It was only after he faced up to the reality that he was an alcoholic that things began to turn around for him. He began attending college again and rediscovered his artistic talent.

Today, John Callahan is proud of his accomplishments. He has said, "I get a sense of fulfillment that keeps me going. I see reasons for the things I've lived through."[114]

Who are you? Discover that, and you will have gained critical information about what you are to do in life.

Who is God? Discern that, and you'll know why.

Leadership is recognizing that people need an environment where they can be nice to themselves.

Give me the knowledge I'll need to be the king of this great nation of yours.

2 Chronicles 1:10 CEV

*P*eter Chan is a master gardener. He left China in the mid-1960s and immigrated to Portland, Oregon, where he bought a modest ranch-style home. His garden is a masterpiece. It is filled with hundreds of different plant species—flowers, perennials, shrubs, vegetables, lawns, and fruit trees—located along beautiful paths and around sparkling pools. All have been artistically positioned and painstakingly maintained.

One day, a friend who was walking through Peter's garden with him asked, "How do you find time to manage all of these plants and all of this growth?"

Peter frowned and said, "You do not manage plants. You coach them, and let them reach their potential."[115]

A good manager knows that the best approach is to hire good people, and then create a nurturing environment in which they can exercise their unique talents to the best of their ability. Most people want to learn, grow, produce, and achieve.

To be a winner in whatever field you choose, find and cultivate good Christian friends, and then do your best to bring out their best spiritual gifts and talents. With a little encouragement, you can all do great things!

■　　■　　■

The . . . leader fosters action, independence, and interdependence in subordinates, not dependence. They are taught to be autonomous so they achieve for their own reasons.

He who believes in Me, the works that I do he will do also; and greater works than these he will do.

John 14:12 *NKJV*

*I*n 1985, Wilma Mankiller became the first woman to be elected Principal Chief of the Cherokee Nation. Many attributed her victory to her having helped found the Cherokee Nation Community Development Department. This organization sought ways to implement renewal projects in rural Cherokee communities. One of their greatest achievements was the Bell Project.

Bell, Oklahoma, was a poor community with about 350 people, 95 percent of them Cherokee. One out of four people living in Bell had to haul water from a well for household use. Almost half of the homes fell below minimum housing standards. Young people left the town to go elsewhere as soon as they possibly could.

The Community Development Department organized community volunteers to install a new water system. Twenty homes and the community center were rehabilitated by the townspeople themselves, who also helped build twenty-five new energy-efficient homes.

Interdependence and the willingness to pitch in saved the community. Mankiller said, "Where everyone expected failure, self-help brought success."[116]

Give others room to grow and achieve their own dreams. Each of us must fulfill our own destiny.

The real measure of a man's worth is how much he would be worth if he lost all his money.

If you want to be perfect, go, sell your possessions and give to the poor, and you will have treasure in heaven. Then come, follow me.

Matthew 19:21

*S*everal years ago, a man was unexpectedly fired from a midsize newspaper. He was stunned—out on the street with only a couple of months' severance pay. After a few days of staring into space, he began to send copies of his résumé and samples of his work to papers that were bigger and more respected than the one he had been fired from.

In the third week, a friend called. Several months earlier, he had helped this woman and her husband move from an apartment to a new home. She was an editor for an exclusive magazine aimed at the ultrarich.

The assignment she offered him was to go to Switzerland, fly first-class, stay in four-star hotels, and eat in four-star restaurants. Not only would all of his expenses be paid, but he'd be given $2,300 for an article on how to live like a millionaire in Switzerland.

While preparing for the trip, he received a job offer from one of the best newspapers in the state. He started there, at better pay, the day after he returned from Switzerland.[117]

It is said that when you have nothing left but God, you have more than enough to start again. Don't confuse your material value with your eternal worth.

Success . . . has nothing to do with what you gain . . . or accomplish for yourself. It's what you do for others.

Whatever you did for one of the least of these brothers of mine, you did for me.

Matthew 25:40

When Mary-Pat Hoffman read about a girl named Maria who had lost both her legs in the Bosnia-Herzegovina war, her heart went out to her. She wrote Maria an upbeat letter, telling her about the fun she had had riding horseback, dancing, and bicycling—all with an artificial leg that she had received at age fourteen.

Mary-Pat offered to buy Maria a pair of new shoes, and pledged to take her daughter along on the shopping trip so the shoes would be "cool."

To her surprise, she heard back from a prosthetics firm that was helping Maria: Maria was scheduled for a press conference in a few days and shoes would be greatly appreciated. Mary-Pat sent two pairs of shoes, hair ornaments, an assortment of socks, and a purse. She also went to the press conference.

As she watched Maria walking on her prosthetic legs, Mary-Pat felt a bond that bypassed any language barrier. Mary-Pat has said: "Maria helped me connect once again with the frightened fourteen-year-old I had been so long ago and appreciate her courage—perhaps for the very first time." The gift Mary-Pat gave became a gift she received.[118]

The old saying is true: Your life is a gift from God. What you do with it is your gift back to Him.

The fullness or emptiness of life will be measured by the extent to which a man feels that he has an impact on the lives of others.

How can we thank God enough for you in return for all the joy that we feel before our God because of you?

1 Thessalonians 3:9 NRSV

A man named Jeffrey went to the movies one night. While he was standing in line at the concession stand, he turned to the man behind him and said, "Say, you look like a nice guy. I'd like to buy you some popcorn."

"What do you mean?" the man asked, suspicious.

"Just that," Jeffrey replied. "I'd like to buy you some popcorn. It would make me feel good."

The man said, "Well, okay, I guess."

At that, the next man in line said, "Hey, wait a minute. What's the matter with me? Don't I look like a nice guy? Why don't you buy me some popcorn?"

Jeffrey hesitated for a moment and then said, "Well, why not? You probably are a nice guy. Okay, I'll buy you some popcorn, too."

"Well, if you buy me popcorn, I'm going to buy you a Coke," the man said.

"Oh yeah?" Jeffrey said. "Then you'd better make it a LARGE Coke."

The three men ended up laughing and joking until they finally reached the head of the line, at which point the man behind the counter said, "You guys are all nuts! I'm the assistant manager, and just for giving me a good laugh today, I'm going to give you all popcorn and Cokes on the house!"[119]

Do something spontaneously nice for someone today. The joy you get in return is truly a gift from God!

■ ■ ■

Acknowledgments

The publisher would like to honor and acknowledge the following individuals for the quotes used in this book: Charles Schulz (8), Lou Holtz (10), Michael Jordan (12), Walt Keisling, Pittsburgh Steelers coach, to Johnny Unitas in 1955 (14), William Blake (16), Yogi Berra (18), John Maxwell (20,54,142), Malcolm Forbes (22), Dale Carnegie (24), Van Crouch (26,70,266,282), Rotary International Motto (30), John Wooden (32), Sam Rayburn (34), Hyman G. Rickover (36), D. L. Moody (38,208), Martin Luther King, Jr. (40), David Starr Johnson (42), Frederick K. C. Price (44), Abraham Lincoln (46), Mike Singletary (48), George S. Patton (50,84), William J. Mayo (52), Dwight Thompson (56), Henry David Thoreau (58,74), Dr. Heartsill Wilson (60), Albert Einstein (62), Walt Disney (64), Richard M. De Vos (66), Dexter Yager (68), Woodrow Wilson (72), Ben Feldman (76), Oliver Wendell Holmes (78,88,202), Jim Valvano (80), Ben Franklin (82), Thomas J. Barlow (86), M. E. Dodd (90), Dr. Robert Schuller (92), Zig Ziglar (94), Ronald Reagan (96,136), Vince Lombardi (98), Don Shula (100), Mike Ditka (102), Joe Lewis (104), Abigail Van Buren (106), Charles E. Jones (108,114,144,158), Larry Bird (110), Goethe (112), T. Boone Pickens (116), W. C. Fields (118), Art Holst (120), Jim Elliot (122), Colonel Sanders (124), Henry Drummond (126), Henry Ford (128), Will Rogers (130), John H. Holcomb (132), Arthur Goldberg (134), Jeanne Robertson (138), Buddy Ryan (140), Sandy Koufax (146), O. G. Mandino (148), Joe Paterno (150), Albert E. N. Gray (152), Robert Frost (154), Andrew Carnegie (156), Lester Sumrall (160), Kenneth Blanchard (162), Mark H. McCormack (164,214), Denis Waitley (166), B. C. Forbes (168,288), Plato (170), Ralph Waldo Emerson (172), Ezra Taft Benson (174), Winston Churchill (176), Kingman Brewster (178,310), Andy Granatelli (180), James L. Hayes (182,240), Ann Landers (184,226), Charles F. Kettering (186), Jean Jacque Rousseau (188), Norman Vincent Peale (190,270), Andre Dawson (192), Charles Schwab (194), Bill Cosby (196), Robert S. McGee (198), David Campbell (200), Thomas J. Winninger (204), John Ruskin (206), James Dobson (210), Bruce Barton (212), Lawrence D. Bell (216), Aristotle (218), Howard W. Newton (220), Willa A. Foster (222), Larry Burkett (224), Helen Keller (228), J. Paul Getty (230), George L. Clements (232), Philip Caldwell (234), Al McGuire (236), John W. Teets (238), John Haggai (242,286), Red Auerbach (244), Gerald R. Ford (246), Tom Landry (248), Stirling Moss (250), Grenville Kleiser (252), Harold Geneen (254), George Bernard Shaw (256), Baron de Coubertin (260), John Brodie (262), Mike Murdock (264), Bill Marriott, Sr. (266), Victor Frankl (272), William James (274,276), Theodore Roosevelt (278), Bobb Biehl (280), John W. Gardner (282), Warren Bennis and Bert Nanus (290), Ty Boyd (292), Billy Sunday (294), John Kenneth Galbraith (296), Peter Drucker (298), William Bernbach (300), Tom Haggai (302), Christopher Hegarty (304), Harold J. Smith (306), Danny Thomas (308).

Endnotes

1 *Encyclopedia of 7700 Illustrations,* Paul Lee Tan (Rockville, MD: Assurance Publishers, 1979), p. 1646.

2 *Encyclopedia of Sermon Illustrations,* David F. Burgess (St. Louis, MO: Concordia Publishing House, 1984), p. 64.

3 *Illustrations Unlimited,* James S. Hewett, ed. (Wheaton, IL: Tyndale House Publishers, 1988), p. 156.

4 *Encyclopedia of Sermon Illustrations,* David F. Burgess (St. Louis, MO: Concordia Publishing House, 1984), p. 150.

5 *Encyclopedia of 7700 Illustrations,* Paul Lee Tan (Rockville, MD: Assurance Publishers, 1979), p. 933.

6 Ibid., p. 1388.

7 Ibid., p. 776.

8 Ibid., p. 943.

9 *Illustrations for Preaching and Teaching,* Craig Brian Larson (Grand Rapids, MI: Baker Books, 1993), p. 276.

10 *Illustrations Unlimited,* James S. Hewett, ed. (Wheaton, IL: Tyndale House Publishers, 1988), p. 160.

11 *Encyclopedia of 7700 Illustrations,* Paul Lee Tan (Rockville, MD: Assurance Publishers, 1979), p. 944.

12 Ibid., p. 949.

13 Ibid., p. 7682.

14 *The Treasury of Inspirational Anecdotes, Quotations, and Illustrations,* E. Paul Hovey, ed. (Grand Rapids, MI: Fleming H. Revell, 1959), p. 215.

15 *Illustrations Unlimited,* James S. Hewett, ed. (Wheaton, IL: Tyndale House Publishers, 1988), p. 174.

16 *Encyclopedia of 7700 Illustrations,* Paul Lee Tan (Rockville, MD: Assurance Publishers, 1979), p. 1374.

17 *Living Faith,* Jimmy Carter (NY: Random House, 1996), pp. 194-195.

18 *Secrets for Success and Happiness,* Og Mandino (NY: Ballantine, 1995), pp. 83-84.

19 *First Things First,* Steven R. Covey, A. Roger Merrill, and Rebecca R. Merrill (NY: Simon and Schuster, 1994), pp. 138-139.

20 *The Critical Edge,* Hendrie Weisinger (Boston: Little, Brown & Co., 1989), pp. 250-251.

21 *First Things First,* Steven R. Covey, A. Roger Merrill, Rebecca R. Merrill (NY: Simon and Schuster, 1994), p. 234.

22 *Pathways to Performance*, Jim Clemmer (Rocklin, CA: Prima Publishing, 1995), p. 38.

23 *What Makes the Great Great,* Dennis P. Kimbro (NY: Doubleday, 1997), p. 133.

24 *Travels*, Michael Crichton (NY: Alfred A. Knopf, 1988), pp. 137-138.

25 *The Leader in You*, Stuart R. Levine and Michael A. Crom (NY: Simon and Schuster, 1993), pp. 153-154.

26 *What Makes the Great Great*, Dennis P. Kimbro (NY: Doubleday, 1997), p. 164.

27 Ibid., p. 176.

28 Ibid., p. 181.

29 *Managing to Have Fun*, Matt Weinstein (NY: Simon and Schuster, 1996), p. 109.

30 *It's Not Over Until You Win!*, Les Brown (NY: Simon and Schuster, 1997), pp. 211-212.

31 *The Speaker's Sourcebook,* Glenn Van Ekeren (Englewood Cliffs, NJ: Prentice Hall, 1988), pp. 120-121.

32 *Pathways to Performance*, Jim Clemmer (Rocklin, CA: Prima Publishing, 1995), p. 199.

33 *The Soul of the Firm*, C. William Pollard (NY: Harper Business (Harper Collins and Zondervan Publishing House, 1966), p. 136.

34 *The Business Bible*, Rabbi Wayne Dosick (NY: William Morrow & Co., 1993), p. 95.

35 *Heart of Wisdom*, Bernard S. Raskas (NY: The Burning Bush Press, 1962), p. 54.

36 *The Achievers*, Raymond C. Johnson (NY: E. P. Dutton, 1987), p. 204.

37 *Everyone's a Coach*, Don Shula and Ken Blanchard (MI: Zondervan Publishing House, 1995), p. 113.

38 *Managing to Have Fun*, Matt Weinstein (NY: Simon and Schuster, 1996), pp. 14-15.

39 *The 7 Habits of Highly Effective People*, Steven R. Covey (NY: Simon and Schuster, 1989), p. 287.

40 *The Little, Brown Book of Anecdotes*, Clifton Fadiman, ed. (Boston: Little, Brown & Co., 1985), p. 157.

41 *The Business Bible,* Rabbi Wayne Dosick (NY: William Morrow & Co., 1993), pp. 28-29.

42 *The Speaker's Sourcebook*, Glenn Van Ekeren (Englewood Cliffs, NJ: Prentice Hall, 1988), pp. 340-341.

43 *Confidence Course*, Walter Anderson (NY: Harper Collins Publishers, 1997), p. 187.

44 *Finding the Champion Within*, Bruce Jenner with Mark Seal (NY: Simon and Schuster, 1996), pp. 13-15.

45 *The Language of Love*, Gary Smalley and John Trent (NY: Simon and Schuster, 1991), pp. 55-57.

46 *Finding the Champion Within,* Bruce Jenner with Mark Seal (NY: Simon and Schuster, 1996), pp. 112-113.

47 *Everyone's a Coach,* Don Shula and Ken Blanchard (MI: Zondervan Publishing House, 1995), p. 33.

48 *Heart of Wisdom,* Bernard S. Raskas (NY: The Burning Bush Press, 1962), p. 28.

49 *The Business Bible,* Rabbi Wayne Dosick (NY: William Morrow & Co., 1993), pp. 52-54.

50 Ibid., pp. 49-50.

51 *All I Really Need to Know I Learned in Kindergarten,* Robert Fulghum (NY: Random House, 1988), pp. 153-155.

52 *The Winner Within*, Pat Riley (NY: G. P. Putnam's Sons, 1993), pp. 124-135.

53 *The New Dynamics of Winning*, Denis Waitley (NY: William Morrow & Co., 1993), pp. 106-107.

54 *The 100% Solution*, Mark H. McCormack (NY: Random House, 1991), pp. 22-23.

55 *Mean Business*, Albert J. Dunlap with Bob Andelman (NY: Random House, 1996), pp. 232-233.

56 *Empires of the Mind,* Denis Waitley (NY: William Morrow & Co., 1995), pp. 139-140.

57 *The Little, Brown Book of Anecdotes*, Clifton Fadiman, ed. (Boston: Little, Brown & Co., 1985), p. 544.

58 *From Bad Beginnings to Happy Endings,* Ed Young (Nashville, TN: Thomas Nelson Publishers, 1994), p. 23.

59 *All I Really Need to Know I Learned in Kindergarten*, Robert Fulghum (NY: Random House, 1988), pp. 165-166.

60 *Pathways to Performance,* Jim Clemmer (Rocklin, CA: Prima Publishing, 1995), pp. 188-189.

61 *Everyone's a Coach,* Don Shula and Ken Blanchard (MI: Zondervan Publishing House, 1995), pp. 171-172.

62 *Finish Strong,* Richard G. Capen, Jr. (San Francisco: Harper Collins 1996), p. 20.

63 *The Path,* Laurie Beth Jones (NY: Hyperion, 1996), pp. 104-105.

64 *Finding the Champion Within*, Bruce Jenner with Mark Seal (NY: Simon and Schuster, 1996), p. 202.

65 *Empires of the Mind*, Denis Waitley (NY: William Morrow & Co., 1995), p. 220.

66 *The Little, Brown Book of Anecdotes*, Clifton Fadiman, ed. (Boston: Little, Brown & Co., 1985), p. 8.

67 *Living Faith*, Jimmy Carter (NY: Random House, 1996), pp. 75-76.

68 *TeamThink*, Don Martin (NY: Penguin Books USA, 1993), pp 223-224.

69 *Beware the Naked Man Who Offers You His Shirt*, Harvey Mackay (NY: William Morrow & Co., 1990), pp. 360-361.

70 *Everyone Is Entitled to My Opinion*, David Brinkley (NY: Alfred A. Knopf, 1996), p. 86.

71 *Getting the Best Out of Yourself and Others*, Buck Rodgers with Irv Levey (NY: Harper & Row, 1987), p. 114.

[72] *Reader's Digest*, January 1997, pp. 91-92.

[73] *You Can Have It All,* Mary Kay Ash (Rocklin, CA: Prima Publishing, 1995), pp. 234-235.

[74] *Extraordinary People with Disabilities,* Deborah Kent and Kathryn A. Quinlan (NY: Children's Press, 1996), pp. 163-165.

[75] *Live Your Dreams,* Les Brown (NY: Avon Books, 1992), p. 126.

[76] *Extraordinary People with Disabilities*, Deborah Kent and Kathryn A. Quinlan (NY: Children's Press, 1996), pp. 213-215.

[77] *Out of the Blue,* Mark Victor Hansen and Barbara Nichols (NY: Harper Collins, 1996), pp. 128-129.

[78] *Dig Your Well Before You're Thirsty,* Harvey Mackay (NY: Doubleday, 1990), p. 62.

[79] *Pathways to Performance*, Jim Clemmer (Rocklin, CA: Prima Publishing, 1995), p. 207.

[80] *The Wisdom of Teams,* Jon R. Katzenbach and Douglas K. Smith (Boston: Harvard Business School Press, 1993), pp. 259-262.

[81] *Illustrations Unlimited,* James Hewett (Wheaton, IL: Tyndale House Publishers, 1988), pp. 123-124.

[82] *Go for the Magic,* Pat Williams (Nashville, TN: Thomas Nelson Publishers, 1995), pp. 188-190.

[83] *Reader's Digest,* January 1997, pp. 33-34.

[84] *Sharkproof,* Harvey MacKay (NY: Harper Collins Publishers, 1993), pp. 210-211.

[85] *Live Your Dreams,* Les Brown (NY: Avon Books, 1992), pp. 66-67.

[86] *TeamThink,* Don Martin (NY: Penguin Books, 1993), pp. 52-53.

[87] *Live Your Dreams,* Les Brown (NY: Avon Books, 1992), pp. 121-122.

[88] *Extraordinary People with Disabilities,* Deborah Kent and Kathryn A. Quinlan (NY: Children's Press, 1996), pp. 216-219.

[89] *All You Can Do Is All You Can Do,* A. L. Williams (Nashville, TN: Thomas Nelson Publishers, 1988), p. 58.

[90] *6000 Sermon Illustrations,* Elon Foster, ed. (Grand Rapids, MI: Baker Book House, 1992), p. 574.

[91] *Reader's Digest,* January 1997, p. 81.

[92] *Born to Succeed,* Colin Turner (Rockport, MA: Element, 1994), pp. 155-156.

[93] *Reader's Digest,* March 1997, pp. 31-36.

[94] *Go for the Magic,* Pat Williams (Nashville, TN: Thomas Nelson Publishers, 1995), p. 20.

[95] *Extraordinary People with Disabilities,* Deborah Kent and Kathryn A. Quinlan (NY: Children's Press, 1996), pp. 220-225.

[96] *Live Your Dreams,* Les Brown (NY: Avon Books, 1992), pp. 194,186.

[97] *Out of the Blue*, Mark Victor Hansen and Barbara Nichols (NY: Harper Collins, 1996), pp. 33-34.

[98] *Confessions of a Street-Smart Manager,* David Mahoney (NY: Simon and Schuster, 1988), p. 74.

[99] *Travels,* Michael Crichton (NY: Alfred A. Knopf, 1988), p. 150.

[100] *All You Can Do Is All You Can Do,* A. L. Williams (Nashville, TN: Thomas Nelson Publishers, 1988), p. 171.

[101] *Go for the Magic,* Pat Williams (Nashville, TN: Thomas Nelson Publishers, 1995), pp. 111-112.

[102] *The Achievers,* Raymond C. Johnson (NY: E. P. Dutton, 1987), pp. 168-169.

[103] *Reader's Digest,* March 1997, pp. 75-77.

[104] *Living Faith,* Jimmy Carter (NY: Random House, 1996), pp. 173-174.

[105] *Reader's Digest,* January 1997, pp. 34-35.

[106] *How to Think Like a CEO,* D. A. Benton (NY: Warner Books, 1996), pp. 80-81.

[107] *Extraordinary People with Disabilities,* Deborah Kent and Kathryn A. Quinlan (NY: Children's Press, 1996), pp. 209-212.

[108] Ibid., pp. 166-168.

[109] *Swim With the Sharks Without Being Eaten Alive*, Harvey Mackay (NY: William Morrow & Co., 1988), pp. 254-255.

[110] *Reader's Digest*, March 1997, pp. 140-141.

[111] *Live Your Dreams,* Les Brown (NY: Avon Books, 1992), p. 117.

[112] *Seize the Day*, Danny Cox and John Hoover (Hawthorne, NJ: Career Press, 1994), pp. 61-62.

[113] *Illustrations Unlimited,* James S. Hewett, ed. (Wheaton, IL: Tyndale House, 1988), pp. 269,492.

[114] *Extraordinary People with Disabilities,* Deborah Kent and Kathryn A. Quinlan (NY: Children's Press, 1996), pp. 197-199.

[115] *Inside America's Fastest Growing Companies,* M. John Storey (NY: John Wiley & Sons, 1989), p. 127.

[116] *No More Frogs to Kiss*, Joline Godfrey (NY: Harper Business, 1995), p. 70.

[117] *Live Your Dreams*, Les Brown (NY: Avon Books, 1992), pp. 187-188.

[118] *Out of the Blue,* Mark Victor Hansen and Barbara Nichols (NY: Harper Collins, 1996), pp. 124-127.

[119] *Managing to Have Fun*, Matt Weinstein (NY: Simon and Schuster, 1996), pp. 83-84.

Other References:

About the Author

Van Crouch is widely regarded as one of the best and more versatile speakers in America.

As the founder and president of the consulting firm, Van Crouch Communications, Van challenges individuals to achieve excellence in their lives.

After ranking as a consistent sales leader with the American Express Company, Van went on to receive many awards for outstanding performance in the insurance industry and has been a qualifying member of the Million Dollar Round Table.

Van Crouch authored the best-selling books, *Stay in the Game, Staying Power,* and *Winning 101.*

Van is in demand for his thought-provoking seminars and keynote engagements to Fortune 500 companies, government organizations, church groups, and management and sales conventions worldwide.

Van Crouch has the ability to motivate people to raise their level of expectation. He is sure to both inspire and challenge you.

For more information about Van Crouch's seminars, speaking engagements, books, cassette tapes, and videos, contact:

Van Crouch Communications
P.O. Box 320
Wheaton, IL 69189
TEL: 630/682-8300
FAX: 630/682-8305
e-mail: VanCrouch@aol.com

This and other books by Van Crouch are available
from your local bookstore.

Winning 101 (portable)
The C.E.O.'s Little Instruction Book
Staying Power

Honor Books
Tulsa, Oklahoma